Hamlet: The Undiscovered Country

Second Edition

By Steve Roth

...who would fardels bear,
To grunt and sweat under a weary life,
But that the dread of something after death,
The undiscover'd country from whose bourn
No traveller returns, puzzles the will,
And makes us rather bear those ills we have
Than fly to others that we know not of?

Hamlet: The Undiscovered Country
Second Edition

By Steve Roth

ISBN: 978-0-9704702-1-8

Open House
Seattle

For additional resources, visit princehamlet.com.

Table of Contents

A Note on Texts and Line References 7

AUTHOR'S PREFACE
The Gross and Scope of My Opinion 9
    The Source of this Our Watch 10
    His Semblance is His Mirror 11
    How Many Children Had Lady Macbeth? 17
    The Journey Is the Reward 19
    For This Relief Much Thanks 20

A Brief History of Shakespeare and *Hamlet* 22

A *Hamlet* Timeline 24

CHAPTER ONE
How Many Years Had Hamlet the Dane? 25
    The Critics 25
    Sixteene Years Had Hamlet the Dane 27
    The First Quarto 28
    The First Folio 28
    Counting on the Gravedigger 30

Thirty Dozen Moons 30
Noble Dust of Alexander 32
Fortinbras: The Delicate and Tender Prince 32
The Morn and Liquid Dew of Youth 33
Hamlet the Student 34
How Many Years Hath Hamlet the Play? 35
Amleth and the Ur-Hamlet 36
The Question of Character 37

CHAPTER TWO
Abstract and Brief Chronicles of the Time

Abstract and Brief Chronicles of the Time 39
The Ghost Walks 41
Murder Most Foul 46
O'erhasty Wedding 48
Christmas Break 48
Hamlet's "Monday Morning" 51
The Mousetrap Sequence 52
Ophelia's Closet 54
Ophelia's Many a Day 55
Fortinbras' Promised March 55
Hamlet at Sea 56
Sudden and More Strange Return 56
Ophelia's Flowers 57
The Gravedigger Sequence 58
Tomorrow Is St. Valentine's Day 60
Claudius the Cruel 61
Not Shriving Time Allowed 61
The Burial of Katherine Hamlett 63
Julius Caesar and the Pirates 63
Shrovetide Revels at Court 64
The Christmas Prince 64
Hamlet and Hamnet 66
Puzzling the Will 67

CHAPTER THREE
A Certain Convocation of Politic Worms

A Certain Convocation of Politic Worms 69
Go Not to Mine Uncle's Bed 70

Something Is Rotten in the State of Denmark 71
Hamlet the Heir 72
Chiefest Courtier, Cousin, and Our Son 75
Return to Wittenberg... 75
The Pate of a Politician 76
The Very Cunning of the Scene 77
Chameleon's Dish.. 80
Denmark's a Prison.. 81
Counselor Most Secret and Most Grave.. 82
Sweet Nymph.. 83
Conception Is a Blessing 87
Oh, Wonderful Son 88
The Imperial Jointress of this War-Like State............................... 90
The Morn and Liquid Dew of Youth... 92

CHAPTER FOUR
The Age Is Grown So Pick'd 95
The Heel of the Courtier 95
The Lord Chamberlain's Men... 97
Shakespeare and The University Wits 100
The Parnassus Plays 103
Hamlet the Player 107
His Picture in Little 109
Th' Expectation and Rose of The Fair State.................................. 110

CHAPTER FIVE
Bear Hamlet Like a Soldier 111
The Greatest Honor.. 111
The Undiscover'd Country 114
To Act, To Do, and To Perform.. 116
Hamlet, Revenge!... 118
Murder Most Foul 119
What Happens in the Mousetrap 120
As Kill a King... 122
Where's Your Father?... 124
When Honor's at the Stake 124

APPENDIX A
A Tragicall Hystorie of Hamlet's Age 129
   The Critics Speak... 132

APPENDIX B
Hamlet, Parnassus, **and the War of the Theaters** 135
   A Clown's Head 136
   Giving the Poets a Pill 137
   The Croaking Raven Doth Bellow for Revenge...................................... 141

APPENDIX C
Thirty Dozen Moons: How Many Years Had Gertrude the Queen? 145
   The Marriage of Frederick II of Denmark..................................... 146
   The Oxford/Cecil Connection 147

APPENDIX D
Shakespeare, the Calendar, the Catholics, and The Stars.............. 151
   Calendar Reform and the Catholic Threat................................... 153
   Shakespeare and the Catholic Calendar 153
   Hamlet and the Infinite Universe... 155
   Astronomical Language in *Hamlet* 157

APPENDIX E
Yond Same Star That's Westward from the Pole............................ 159
   Cepheus Rising 163

APPENDIX F
The Drowning of Katherine Hamlett 167
   To Act, To Do, To Perform 168
   Maimed Rites 170
   A Dead Woman in Tiddington... 171

About the Author.. 174

A Note on Texts
and Line References

Throughout this book there are references to line numbers in *Hamlet* (so you can keep me honest), and to many other sources—primary documents from the Elizabethan age, and secondary commentary from critics and historians over the centuries. Many of these references (all of the line references) are hyperlinked in the ebook version (visit princehamlet.com), so you can jump straight to the web sites where the materials appear. Those hyperlinks are designated with a light dotted underline, so if you're reading the printed book you know whether it's worth your time to open the electronic version to get at the link.

All the line-number references are to the printed *Riverside Shakespeare*, and the modern-spelling quotations are also from the *Riverside*. That fine volume (my desert-island book) offers a great text (though its modernization is somewhat idiosyncratic), beautifully produced, plus excellent footnotes, textual notes, and fascinating supplementary materials. The line-reference hyperlinks, however, will take you to the 1914 Oxford Shakespeare text on Bartelby.com. You'll find that the text in *Oxford* doesn't exactly match the *Riverside* references cited in this book; every edition of *Hamlet* is different.

I link to the Oxford text because the *Riverside* electronic text is not publicly available, and when this was written the Oxford edition was the best modern-spelling text freely available on the web. It's far superior to the "Moby" text on most Shakespeare sites. The Oxford text also has line numbers embedded in the HTML, so the line-reference links will take you straight to the line being discussed. (Aficionados might prefer David Bevington's modern-spelling edition at Internet Shakespeare Editions, or Jesus Tronch's modern-spelling "enfolded" edition at hamletworks.org.)

There are some places where I've linked directly to one of the original source editions for the play (First Quarto, Second Quarto, or First Folio). The line references use "through line numbers" (see below); the links take you to the wonderful Internet Shakespeare Editions collection.

If you'd like to see the First Folio and Second Quarto editions conflated together—making it easy to compare the two—run don't walk to the Enfolded Hamlet on hamletworks.org. (Click "Browse Hamlet Works," then "Linked Enfolded Hamlet.") This magisterial "variorum" edition also lets you view centuries of commentary that has been written about any line in the play, by clicking on each line number. (Just one example: the commentary on Hamlet's "too too solid flesh" line 1.2.129 runs to twenty-four pages, single-spaced.)

Not surprisingly, the line numbers for all these editions don't jibe. Not only do the texts vary markedly, but they use different numbering methods. The 1914 Oxford, for instance, counts a whole paragraph of prose as one line, while *Riverside* numbers prose lines according to its own line breaks. The electronic Folio and Quarto texts are numbered from the beginning of the play to the end ("through line numbers," or TLNs, based on the First Folio lineation), not broken up by act and scene. The Enfolded Hamlet offers both TLNs and act-scene-line numbering.

In a few cases I needed to link to an actual facsimile page in the First Folio. The whole darn thing is available in living color at the Furness Collection and at the aforementioned Internet Shakespeare Editions.

For references to materials that aren't available on the web, I've tried to provide enough information that you can find it easily using a web search or—*in extremis* (i.e. materials on microfilm)—the online catalog of a good academic library. Let me know if I've missed any citations or links, if you find any broken links, or if you have any other comments on the book: steve@princehamlet.com.

The Gross and Scope
of My Opinion

It's traditional to begin this preface with the obligatory question: After 400 years, is there anything left to say about *Hamlet*? It's equally obligatory—with 170-odd pages between these words and the back cover—to answer in the affirmative. It's probably easiest to quote one of *Hamlet*'s greatest editors, as he pays homage to another. In his 1982 Arden *Hamlet*, Harold Jenkins says, "Like Dover Wilson before me, I have been surprised at how many passages in Shakespeare still lack satisfactory exegesis." In other words—even after twenty-eight years preparing his edition—he still hasn't managed to explain a lot of the jokes.

It's also traditional to say here that each generation creates its own *Hamlet*. That's true; this book reflects thinking and sensibilities that might not have occurred to earlier generations. But that view is also wrong, because our generation isn't just seeing *Hamlet* from a new perspective. We *know* more about *Hamlet* than our predecessors did. (Another, and I hope final, necessary traditionalism: "*they* are what we know.") We understand more about Elizabethan beliefs regarding ghosts and religion (various and contradictory). There's been great work exploring Elizabethan views of medicine, botany, astronomy, rhetoric, and much else. We know more about how plays were staged, and how they were published. Anti-Stratfordian authorship contrarians notwithstanding, we know a heck of a lot more about Shakespeare and his time than scholars did fifty or a hundred years ago.

Beyond these kinds of facts, though, we also have interpretations and insights that have arisen over the centuries, some of which are irrefutably true, and which earlier generations didn't have benefit of. One example: John Dover Wilson pointed out in 1935 that when Lucianus poisons Gonzago in the mousetrap play, Hamlet has just announced that Lucianus is nephew to the king. So the courtiers don't see a representation of Claudius' crime (they don't even know about the murder); they see a nephew murdering his uncle the king, in a play put on by the current king's nephew! That insight is just plain true, and imparts an accurate understanding of the play that wasn't there before. (See Chapter Five for more on this mousetrap business.)

So there's a lot left to know about *Hamlet*, and a lot left to say that hasn't been said before. As the seminal text of the humanist religion, it shows every sign of being bottomless. Hamlet himself probably best answers those who would presume to think otherwise: 3.2.264

> "Why, look you now, how unworthy a thing you make of me. You would play upon me; you would seem to know my stops; you would pluck out the heart of my mystery; you would sound me from my lowest note to the top of my compass."

My aspirations are hardly so lofty. But I have some hope of adding to what we know, and perhaps speaking a word for my generation.

The Source of this Our Watch

It wasn't until I'd almost finished writing this book that I realized how long it had been growing in me. Going through my old college copy of the *Riverside Shakespeare*, I came on a note I penned twenty-five years ago—a comment on the gravedigger's line that pegs Hamlet as a thirty-year-old. That line bothered me then, and over the ensuing years it kept bothering me—to the point that I started digging through the centuries of commentary on the play, wondering if others had been similarly troubled. (They had.) For all those years, I've assaulted anyone I could get to listen with my thoughts on the subject.

Eventually all that reading, pondering, and brooding came to a head. I finally said to my wife one Saturday morning, "I'm leaking," and started writing. This book began as an article on the (seemingly) simple subject of Hamlet's age, and distended into the fixation you're reading now.

Hamlet's age seems like a trivial problem, but like so many things in this tapestry of a play, as you start to unravel the threads of the question, it reveals overlapping, interrelated layers and nuances of sense, meaning, and import. And as I dug even deeper, to my true surprise the question yielded new discoveries about the play—some just interesting, some perhaps significant—that have lain hidden within it for four hundred years.

His Semblance is His Mirror

If there's one thing that's truly remarkable about *Hamlet* (and great literature in general), it's the play's seemingly infinite complexity and coherence. Everywhere you look there are reflections (and reflexions), echoes, allusions, and interrelated cross-correlations. It's an endless interweave whose only equal for me is the complexity of the human mind. That's why the simple problem that launched this project—the question of Hamlet's age—turned into a whole book: if you start teasing at one thread, it eventually connects to every other. And those threads connect outside the play in myriad copulas. My pleasure comes from following those threads—from unpacking that density.

I have to admit that one thing I greatly enjoy is explaining some of the remarkably involved in-jokes that litter the play, and "puzzle the will." This punch-line approach sounds trivial, but (in addition to being fun) it's actually an important touchstone for whether a given interpretation, criticism, or insight is valid—does it explain the jokes? (This also points to what's wrong with so many stage and film productions of this play—which is arguably Shakespeare's most amusing in its multi-level irony: *they're not funny*.)

This book is written for everyday readers and Shakespeare enthusiasts, both professionals and amateurs. Scholars will, I hope, excuse my going over familiar ground that will not be familiar to the everyday reader. And everyday readers will, I hope, excuse my occasional obfuscatory nod to the scholars; sometimes I couldn't resist.

Speaking of scholars, I need to briefly note here that while I have great interest in literary theory, I have little interest in most of the currently fashionable schools of literary "Theory." To quote David Cressy, one of the best historians writing today, "It is not necessary to invoke terms like hierarchical inversion, theatrical mimesis, reaffirmative reintegration, liminal transgression, or latent control, to demonstrate that Shrovetide was a time for letting off steam." (*Bonfires and Bells*, 18)

But as someone has aptly noted, people who say they don't pay attention to theory really don't know what their theory is. So it's probably best to state my prejudices here. If you were to put me in any critical "camp," you could probably best describe my approach as post-new-historicist neo-formalism, which I guess makes me a New New New New Critic. For those who understand that joke, a kudos. For others, here are some of my key beliefs.

Prejudice #1. If I can't make sense of something, the problem is most likely with me, not the play. I'm not saying Shakespeare was perfect; there are things in *Hamlet* that just don't make sense. But the coherence of the play is so remarkable—and the more you look, the more coherent it becomes—that I have to start from the assumption that anything that doesn't make sense is my problem, not Will's.

Scholars tend to dismiss discussions of the play that seem to explain the plot or the characters' motivations too neatly, arguing that Shakespeare wasn't so much concerned with credible plots as with effective drama. And they're right; Shakespeare is completely untroubled by improbable plots. The wacky final scenes in *Cymbeline* and *Measure for Measure* don't just strain credulity, they're absurd. Examples are endless. Even the ghost wouldn't have been "credible" to a good chunk of Shakespeare's audience. But credibility isn't the same as coherent narrative and plausible motivation. And coherent narrative, coupled with plausible motivations, is dramatically effective. Shakespeare uses that, just as he uses every other technique that comes to hand. I would argue that he uses it especially well in *Hamlet*.

Prejudice # 2. Analyzing and understanding a poem makes it more beautiful, not less. For me, the platitude "A poem should not mean but be" is little more than a simplistic romanticism. When you discover that "sallied" in "O that this too too sallied flesh would melt,/Thaw and resolve it selfe into a dewe," Q2: 312 was common Elizabethan usage for "sullied," and find that "sallies" is used in exactly that sense in Polonius's directions to Reynaldo, Q2: 932 does that damage or enrich your experience of the play? It gets even richer when you learn that Elizabethan pronunciation further emphasizes the *double-entendre* of "sullied" and "solid."

Way back in my undergraduate classes and before, I learned that you have to first get at the sense of a poem—what does it *say*? Without that basic understanding, you can't perceive its full beauty. That's my main goal in this book: to get at what the play actually tells us about the events, characters, and relationships. From that platform, you can stretch to the higher ramparts of meaning, import, and implication.

Prejudice #3. *Hamlet* is not just a drama to be played, but literature to be read. One of the greater ironies of Shakespeare scholarship over the last century is the ongoing effort by Shakespeare scholars—most of whom spend dozens of hours a week enjoining, cajoling, and browbeating their students into addressing Shakespeare's plays as literature—to deny that those plays are literature. Shakespeare, these scholars say, thought of his plays as disposable, populist ephemera, like Hollywood scripts; they were created for performance, and that's all. Views, interpretations, editions, or theoretical schools which posit a reader are, by this thinking, sadly and anachronistically missing the point.

I think this viewpoint—held even more widely in the theater community, and only recently (and resoundingly) challenged in the scholarly community by Lukas Erne's *Shakespeare as Literary Dramatist*—is silly. At least a dozen of Shakespeare's plays had been published in the 1590s, prior to the 1600/ 1601 debut of *Hamlet* as we know it—at least some of them with Shakespeare's apparent approval. Publishers in Elizabethan times published books for one reason: because they could sell them at the shops in St. Paul's churchyard. And people bought them to read—not as prompt books for their home theaters.

Shakespeare also published his then-bestselling works—the narrative poems *Venus and Adonis* and *The Rape of Lucrece*—in 1593/1594. These were written and published for reading, silently or aloud. And his sonnets—which were patently for reading—were circulating in manuscript among his friends throughout the late 1590s (they weren't published until 1609). Shakespeare clearly knew when he wrote *Hamlet* that his works were not just performed, but were widely read. And they were read by his best customers—courtiers, inns-of-court men, and others who populated the higher-ticket galleries of the Globe Theater, the stage seats at Blackfriars, and the most coveted seats: where Shakespeare's company played before the queen at court.

Add to this the repeated injunction from Shakespeare's long-time friends and colleagues Heminges and Condell in their introduction "To the Great Variety of Readers" in the 1623 First Folio collection of Shakespeare's plays: "Read him therefore, and again, and again." Fl Facs. p. 8 (Equally revealing but more amusing is their earlier injunction: "But, whatever you do, Buy.") The opening page of the Folio is an epistle by Ben Jonson titled "To the Reader." It's clear that the plays were not just for playing, but for reading.

So the arguments you sometimes hear—that these complex interrelation-ships within the play can't have any validity, because nobody watching a play could possibly catch them—are just foolish. Even the great Shakespeare scholar John Dover Wilson falls for this angle, but in a contradictory way. He agrees, right at the beginning of *What Happens in Hamlet*, that no audience member could catch all the complexity:

> There is, for instance, Hamlet's quibbling, much of it, with double or triple point, beyond the comprehension of even the nimblest-witted groundlings. Its existing proves that Shakespeare could count upon a section of the audience at the Globe, nobles, inns-of-court men and the like, capable in swiftness of apprehension and sustained attention of almost any subtlety he cared to put them to, and moreover armed like Hamlet himself with their 'tables' to set down matters which they could not at once understand or wished especially to remember.

The tables Wilson refers to are the widely used pocket tables, or table books, made of erasable waxed cardboard leaves, or "tablets," with a brass stylus attached. (Think: Palm Pilots without the batteries.) Hamlet refers to them after the ghost's revelation: "Yea, from the table of my memory/I'll wipe away all trivial fond records…" 1.5.106 A few lines later he jokes wryly on them, with a nod to the galleries and the wits at court: "My tables—meet it is I set it down/That one may smile, and smile, and be a villain!" He jibes on them again in his ridicule, in the First Quarto edition of the play, of a clownish player who "keeps one suit of jests, as a man is known by one suit of apparel," so "gentlemen quote his jests down in their tables, before they come to the play." Q1: 1896

Or take for another instance this line from the _Parnassus_ plays, a trilogy
written and produced by Cambridge students in the same years as *Hamlet.*
Gullio, a parody of aristocratic patrons, is misquoting love poetry and
threatening more. Ingenioso, an acerbic poet, says in an exasperated aside,
"We shall have nothing but pure Shakespeare, and shreds of poetry that he
hath gathered at the theaters."

Wilson's insight into Shakespeare's audience is incredibly useful—there
was a large contingent of brilliantly educated individuals who paid very close
attention, even writing down favorite passages for later thought, discussion,
and misquotation. Shakespeare was not just writing for a pack of witless
groundlings, or just for dramatic effect, as people often claim, but also for
attentive and highly capable listeners and readers. (Even the most cursory
acquaintance with the intricate jibes and counter-jibes that were thrown
about between playwrights in the "poet's war" that came to its head in the
Fall of 1601 will make clear that the poets were very much also writing for
each other.) Shakespeare's ability to write for apprentices and earls, for court
and for courtyard, for the stage *and* the page, constitutes an important part
of—and demonstration of—the mastery that has transformed him into
"Shakespeare."

But in Appendix F of Wilson's book, where he takes occasion to savage
Salvadore de Madariaga's *On Hamlet,* he takes an opposite and ill-consid-
ered tack in his eagerness to embay his Spanish rival:

> This is to read *Hamlet* like a book, a historical monograph or a per-
> sonal record such as the *Autobiography* of Benvenuto Cellini, in-
> stead of being, as it was and is, an elaborate work of dramatic
> art…the only criticism relevant to such an art is one that follows
> these impressions in the order in which the dramatist released
> them, and then considers the total impression left behind upon the
> audience after the play is finished….to begin in the middle and
> then jump forwards and backwards…is like looking down at St
> Paul's from an aeroplane instead of from the ground, which was
> the only perspective Wren had in view.

This is, indeed, to read *Hamlet* like a book, as many of Will's better-bred
contemporaries did. No audience member watching from beginning to end
could possibly cross-correlate all the scattered descriptions of Hamlet's sea

journey, for instance—the sailor's words, Hamlet's letters to Horatio 4.6.8 and
to Claudius, 4.7.49 and Hamlet's later spoken report to Horatio. 5.2.3 But for
those of patient merit, those references come together into an incredibly
coherent story. The cross-correlations forward and backward in the play
make up a huge part of its interest, power, and beauty. Saying that "the only
criticism relevant to such an art is one that follows these impressions in the
order in which the dramatist released them" is patently absurd. (This especially as we have no idea in what order he "released" many of them).

So in the course of this book you'll find me quoting some lines and passages more than once. *Hamlet* being the cross-referential harvest ground
that it is, a single line may serve no less than three dozen avowed purposes,
with spurious interpretations additional. This book is an attempt to tease out
some few of those interrelationships and multiple meanings.

Prejudice #4. It's fruitless to talk about "the author's intentions." There's
no shortage of places in the text where you have to wonder what Shakespeare meant, but in general it's not a useful question. Consider, for instance,
the repeating imagery and ideas in these three passages:

Hamlet speaking of Gertrude: 1.2.154
  O God, a beast that wants discourse of reason
  Would have mourned longer

Hamlet, to Rosencrantz and Guildenstern: 2.2.250
  What piece of work is a man, how noble in reason, how infinite in
  faculties, in form and moving, how express and admirable in action, how like an angel in apprehension, how like a god: the beauty
  of the world; the paragon of animals...

Hamlet, of himself: 4.4.38
  What is a man
  If his chief good and market of his time
  Be but to sleep and feed, a beast, no more:
  Sure he that made us with such large discourse
  Looking before and after, gave us not
  That capability and god-like reason
  To fust in us unused...

Did Shakespeare "intend" all these echoes, scattered throughout the play? On what level of consciousness did he intend them? Was he even consciously aware of them? Which ones? Whatever the answer, he created these echoes and thousands of others, and it's those connections that make the fabric of the play so rich and dense. It doesn't serve any purpose to guess at whether, and on what level, he "intended" them.

Of course you have to rule out anything that the author couldn't possibly have intended on any level of consciousness. (Though poststructuralists will brand me a *naïf* for saying so.) It would be useless and spurious, for instance, to suggest an allusion to something that only appears in "Amleth" legends prior to their telling by Saxo Grammaticus. It's unlikely that Shakespeare even knew Saxo's version, and it's beyond unlikely that he knew the earlier legends.

How Many Children Had Lady Macbeth?

The simplistic distinction between what Shakespeare might have intended and what he could not have masks a much murkier problem. That problem is expressed beautifully in the article which inspired the title of Chapter One: L. C. Knights' seminal 1933 essay, "How Many Children Had Lady Macbeth?" (available in *Explorations,* 1947). His title refers to Lady Macbeth's "I have given suck, and know/How tender 'tis to love the babe that milks me," 1.7.54 and the seemingly irresistible appeal that lures critics to expand on such statements.

Knights takes arms against this tendency in Shakespeare criticism, a tendency that emerged in the eighteenth century and flowered (or in Knights' view grew like a weed) in the Romantic era: the tendency to concentrate on Shakespeare's characters and their "character" as if they were real historical personages. Nowhere is it more evident than in *Hamlet* criticism—the question of Hamlet's character has absorbed more ink than any other.

Knights' position is much similar to mine: that Shakespeare's plays are dramatic poems, and that you have to look at their full effect—poetic, literary, and dramatic—to understand and appreciate them. This effect emerges through character, action, plot, stage directions, rhythm, rhyme, imagery, allusion, and a host of other literary and dramatic constructs. But at bottom, all of these emerge from language, and it's there that you must seek first to understand the play—in the depths of the text.

So I'm with Knights in disdaining the rambling discourses on Shakespeare's noble characters that are scattered through the Romantic era and beyond. (Knights speaks of them as "pseudo-critical investigations that are only slightly parodied by the title of this essay.") Shakespeare's characters are not real people, or our friends, but dramatic, literary, and poetic entities that illuminate our lives and thoughts—and each other's—through their words and actions.

At the same time, in this book I venture into areas that Knights would no doubt have scoffed at. When I surmise that Hamlet's "continual practice" at fencing 5.2.143 must have been with the officers of the guard, and then with the pirates, I'm crossing the line that Knights draws—entering that area of surmise which assumes a world beyond what the play states explicitly. (Knights might have given nodding credence to the evidence from Plutarch that I cite in Chapters One and Five, on young Caesar's time with the pirates and its similarity to Hamlet's.)

But this returns us to the notion of coherence, and authorial intent. It's patently clear to me that Shakespeare conceived a whole world of *Hamlet* (perhaps over a decade or more), most of which he tells us about in the text of the play. There's no other way he could have built the cohesive chronology described in Chapter Two, or coordinated the characters, motivations, and actions of this huge work so convincingly.

But the edges of that world are not sharp and distinct. When Polonius tells Ophelia that he has heard (from some unnamed sources) that Hamlet "hath very oft of late/Given private time to you, and you yourself/Have of your audience been most free and bounteous", 1.3.99 do those audiences become part of that world, worthy of consideration and discussion? Can we surmise that those audiences included fond words between the two? When Hamlet speaks to Horatio of "the circumstance/Which I have told thee of my father's death," 3.2.40 don't we have to assume they have had a conversation that we weren't privy to? Or take Hamlet, Rosencrantz, and Guildenstern's discussion of the Elizabethan "poet's war" between competing playwrights and acting companies. 2.2.254 The text doesn't tell us explicitly that Shakespeare is referring to that war, or actually engaging in a skirmish, but he is certainly doing both.

So ruling out discussion of anything that isn't explicitly stated in the text is a disservice both to the text and to ourselves. The hints, echoes, suggestions, allusions, and connotations in the text are emphatically part of that text. They contribute mightily to the overall literary and dramatic effect that both Knights and I prize most highly.

There's certainly more than one place in this book where I've skirted the imperfect boundary between what Shakespeare might and could not have intended. But I hope I've stayed on the reasonable side of certainty. I was more than tempted in more than one case, for instance, to cite the 1586 sojourn and performances at Elsinore by Kemp, Bryan, and Pope, who by 1594 were members of Shakespeare's company. It's certainly possible that Will was part of their company by that time, and even accompanied them (as an apprentice?) on the trip. It's even more likely that he received direct report from them. But there's absolutely no evidence of either. So there's one lure, at least, that I didn't rise to.

This returns us, finally, to the simple but admittedly not so useful touchstone: what can we reasonably assume, and what's on the far side of improbable? That probability arises, like all true knowledge, not just from the viability of individual facts and statements, but from the context of those statements—the other facts that surround and support them. Does the whole weave of conceit cohere, as *Hamlet* does, into a pattern that rings true both in its whole and in its individual parts?

I like to think that this book meets that test, though I have little doubt that some will think otherwise. They will think that some of my suppositions were "to consider too curiously to consider so," 5.2.86 or that I've gone beyond the pale of probability in some of my conjectures. I'm enthusiastic to hear those opinions. Please don't hesitate to write: steve@princehamlet.com.

The Journey Is the Reward

This book is written in the inductive mode; I have a central thesis—that Hamlet is a teen, not an adult—but the conclusions that arise from that thesis emerge in the course of the argument. I reveal my discoveries in much the order that I came to them. So this book is as much a tale of my journey into the undiscovered country as it is a description of the country arrived at.

That journey is centered on the framework of chronology that is both blatantly obvious and subtly (even deviously) hidden in *Hamlet*. So after exploring the issue of Hamlet's age in Chapter One, in Chapter Two I lay out the whole chronology of the play—who does what and when. Then in the remaining chapters I turn to the really interesting stuff: the implications of those words and actions. What do they tell us about the play, and ultimately about ourselves? In the appendices you'll find more detailed inquiries into some curious areas that I couldn't resist, but that would have clogged up the first five chapters.

For This Relief Much Thanks

I said that when I started writing this book I felt like I was leaking. And I was—badly. But to quote Monty Python, "I'm feeling much better." And for that I must give thanks.

First, to all who came before me. I am not, of course, the first person to enter this labyrinth. This book could not be if it weren't for thousands of critics and commentators who have discovered connections and explanations that had lain unrevealed to others. I am hopelessly indebted to all those critics, and have attempted to give credit where due. But to quote William Minto's 1875 comment on "the mass of Shakespearian literature," "It would take the labor of a lifetime to make quite sure that a particular view had never been expressed before." That mass of literature has grown geometrically since Minto penned those words. And in many areas, large and small, I could not give credit without digressing into history-of-ideas essays covering critical discussions that often spanned decades or centuries.

For all the ideas in this book that others have come upon before me, many thanks. I hope that those in the future will use my ideas with as much enthusiasm as I have received those of my predecessors.

To the late Edmund K. Chambers, who humbly described himself as "one who only plays at scholarship in the rare intervals of a busy administrative life." (His words could have spoken for me as well, when I began this book.) Professor Chambers' two-volume *Medieval Stage,* four-volume *Elizabethan Stage,* and two-volume *William Shakespeare* are the grounds upon which all Shakespeare critics stand—or should stand, at any rate. May flights of angels sing thee to thy rest.

Dozens of people have taken the time to share their thoughts with me in conversations and correspondence. I'd like to offer special thanks to the following, while offering my appreciation and apologies to any who I have failed to include: Mark Alexander, Cindy Bell, Michael Best, Sandra Billington, David Bishop, Tony Burton, Jessica Clark, Nick Clary, Ken Collins,

Hardy Cook, Carol Cullen, Ron Drummond, Gabriel Egan, Glenn Fleishman, Barry Gaines, Christopher Gauntt, Eugene Giddens, Kitty Harmon, Lisa Hopkins, Stephanie Hughes, Dennis James, Norman Kane, John Kerrigan, Manfred Kiefer, Jan Kinrade, Bernice Kliman, Graeme Lindridge, Carol Morley, Toke Norby, Vladimir Pimonov, Anthony Powell, Eric Rasmussen, Rainbow Saari, Matthew Steggle, William Sutton, Jesus Tronch-Perez, Amy Ulen, Malcom Underwood, Peter Usher, Henrika Vuorinen, David Wallace, and Robin Williams.

To my parents, Ben and Betsy Roth. Thanks for teaching me to "read," even though my grade school told you not to teach me how to read.

And most of all to my wonderful girls, Dia and Jesse. Thank you for giving me time and space enough to make this work, and play this play.

A Brief History of Shakespeare and *Hamlet*

This listing includes the most significant dates for Shakespeare and *Hamlet*, plus some other events that are referred to hereafter, for easy reference and recall.

ca. 1200	Saxo Grammaticus's *Gesta Danorum* (with Amleth story) written in Latin.
1514	*Gesta Danorum* published.
1558	Ascension of Elizabeth I.
1564	April 26. Shakespeare baptised.
1570	F. de Belleforest's *Histoires Tragique* (with Amleth story) published in French. Multiple editions through 1582. First known English translation published 1608.
1579	December 17. Katherine Hamlett drowned in the Avon near Stratford. Inquest and subsequent burial, February 11, 1580.
1585	February 2. Hamnet and Judith Shakespeare, Shakespeare's twins, baptised.
1586	Future Chamberlain's Men Kemp, Bryan, and Pope play at Elsinore.
1588	September. Death of Richard Tarleton, preeminent comic actor, clown, and favorite of the queen. His will is dated September 3.
1589	Thomas Nashe makes mock of the "Ur-*Hamlet*" author: "he will afford you whole Hamlets, I should say handfulls of tragical speaches."
1594	June 9. Shakespeare joins the newly formed Chamberlain's Men.
	April. Shakespeare's *Venus and Adonis* published, dedicated to the Earl of Southampton.
	June 9. Ur-*Hamlet* played by Admiral's and Chamberlain's Men at Newington Butts.
1596	August 11. Hamnet Shakespeare buried.
	Ur-*Hamlet* ridiculed by Thomas Lodge: "the ghost which cried so miserably at the Theatre, like an oyster-wife, 'Hamlet, revenge.'"

1598	Sometime (perhaps years) after this year's publication of Specht's *Chaucer*, Gabriel Harvey pens a handwritten marginal note in that edition, "The younger sort takes much delight in Shakespeares Ve nus, & Adonis: but his Lucrece, & his tragedie of Hamlet, Prince of Denmarke, haue it in them, to please the wiser sort."
1599	*Julius Caesar* debuts. Attended by Thomas Platter September 21.
1600	Christmas/New Years 1601. *Return to Parnassus Part I* played at St. John's College, Cambridge. Includes a gravedigger turning up a "clown's head."
1601	September 8. John Shakespeare (Will's father) buried.
	Spring/Fall. Peak of the "poet's war." Jonson's *Poetäster* and Dekker (and Marson's?) *Satiromastix*. The latter (played by the Chamberlain's Men) echoes Lodge's ridicule: "My name's Hamlet's Revenge."
	Fall. First playings of Shakespeare's *Hamlet* as we know it. (Possibly 1600, with revisions Fall 1601; see Appendix A.)
	Christmas/New Years. *Return to Parnussus Part II* played at St. John's College, Cambridge. Includes Burbage and Kempe as characters. Multiple references to Shakespeare, including his giving Jonson a "purge."
1602	July 26. *Hamlet* entered in the Stationer's register. "latelie Acted by the Lo: Chamberleyne his servantes".
1603	First quarto (Q1) of Hamlet published (half the length of, and otherwise much inferior to, later editions).
	March. Queen Elizabeth dies. James VI of Scotland (with his wife, Anne of Denmark) crowned as James I of England and Scotland.
	Chamberlain's Men become King's Men, Shakespeare and other sharers become Grooms of the King's Chamber.
1604	Second quarto (Q2) of Hamlet published. "Newly imprinted and enlarged to almost as much againe as it was, according to the true and perfect Coppie."
1616	April 23. Shakespeare's death.
1623	First Folio (F1) published, with a *Hamlet* quite different from Q2.

A *Hamlet* Timeline

The Chronology of *Hamlet*

Possible Dates

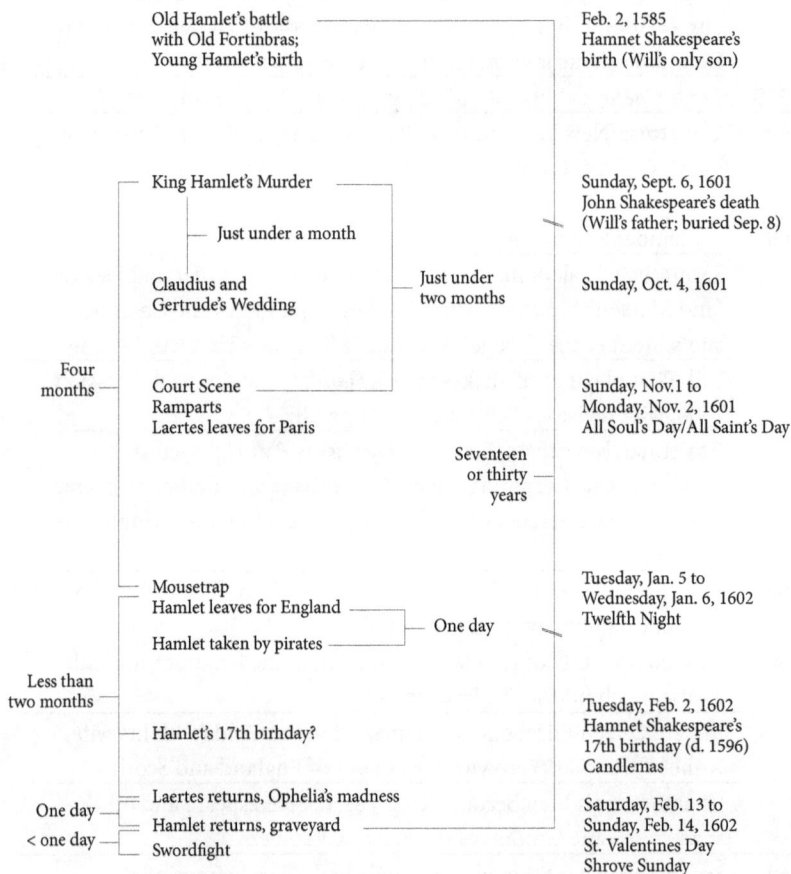

Old Hamlet's battle
with Old Fortinbras;
Young Hamlet's birth

Feb. 2, 1585
Hamnet Shakespeare's
birth (Will's only son)

King Hamlet's Murder

Sunday, Sept. 6, 1601
John Shakespeare's death
(Will's father; buried Sep. 8)

— Just under a month

Claudius and
Gertrude's Wedding

Just under
two months

Sunday, Oct. 4, 1601

Four
months

Court Scene
Ramparts
Laertes leaves for Paris

Sunday, Nov. 1 to
Monday, Nov. 2, 1601
All Soul's Day/All Saint's Day

Seventeen
or thirty
years

Mousetrap
Hamlet leaves for England

Hamlet taken by pirates

One day

Tuesday, Jan. 5 to
Wednesday, Jan. 6, 1602
Twelfth Night

Less than
two months

Hamlet's 17th birhday?

Tuesday, Feb. 2, 1602
Hamnet Shakespeare's
17th birthday (d. 1596)
Candlemas

One day —
< one day —

Laertes returns, Ophelia's madness
Hamlet returns, graveyard
Swordfight

Saturday, Feb. 13 to
Sunday, Feb. 14, 1602
St. Valentines Day
Shrove Sunday

*Visit princehamlet.com for an interactive version of this
chronology with links to supporting text passages.*

CHAPTER ONE

How Many Years Had Hamlet the Dane?

Aside from the two old chestnuts of *Hamlet* criticism—Hamlet's character and Hamlet's delay—probably no other topic has engaged Shakespeare fans more than the thorny problem of his age: is Hamlet sixteen or thirty? Whether you're wandering through classes discussing *Hamlet*, lurking the boards at rehearsal, eavesdropping in the bar after a performance, or perusing the online discussions, you find people of all stripes tangling with this key contradiction.

In two blatant references in the accepted text that most people have read, the gravedigger says Hamlet is thirty. But the original texts are far less definitive (downright contradictory is more like it). And aside from these and two other items in the text, everything else about the play—including the gravedigger himself—contradicts the gravedigger's statements.

The Critics

When I first tackled this problem, the obvious course was to see if the critics had already solved it. Not surprisingly, I'm not the first to dig through these old bones. Every major critic in the last century and a half has noted the oddly obtrusive discrepancy between the gravedigger's lines and the overall impression of Hamlet's youth given throughout the play. At least a dozen critics have addressed the issue, with comments ranging from lengthy discourses to terse footnotes to dismissive asides. You'll find a rundown of their discussions in Appendix A, and transcripts of some commentaries at princehamlet.com.

One twentieth-century critic bears particular mention. Despite quite inveterate searching over the years, I'm delighted to find, some half-dozen years after publishing the first edition of this book, that I have been quite ably preceded in my conclusions here about Hamlet's age. Robert Cohen addressed several of the key issues in 1973, in *Educational Theatre Journal*. In particular, he offers a very good account of the discrepancies in the original printed texts of the play, and in Shakespeare's source for the Hamlet story.

To understand these discussions, it's important to realize that there are actually three texts of *Hamlet*, and that they disagree in many particulars, large and small. In his 1932 *Manuscript of Shakespeare's Hamlet*, J. D. Wilson finds more than 2,000 variants between the two main texts alone—1,300 of which he considers to be "of any importance." Whole speeches are absent from each of those two versions. So a lot of the discussion inevitably centers on whether and when Shakespeare (and/or others) revised the play. Scholarly consensus is nonexistent. But somewhere in that process, these contradictions arose. Some have speculated that the gravedigger's lines were added at some point for Shakespeare's star partner in The Lord Chamberlain's Men, Richard Burbage, who was roughly thirty years old when Shakespeare's *Hamlet* debuted in 1600/1601. (We know Burbage played Hamlet, but we don't know when.) Many other equally unprovable speculations are possible.

We do know this: the Elizabethan theater scene was a lot like Hollywood when it came to scripts. Many were created by more than one writer, and many if not most suffered revision at multiple hands—often when old plays were restaged in later years. And Shakespeare was as savvy as any Hollywood script doctor. When it comes to rewriting key passages for Burbage or any other purpose, you can almost hear the call to the writer echoing down those 400 years: "Script!"

But it's also possible, as explained below, that these thirty-year references ended up in the play inadvertently, in the course of revision, editing, copying, proofreading, and publication.

One important recent discussion is by Professor Harold Bloom, our current defender of the Western canon, modern-day bardolater, and Hamlet eulogist. He evades the question entirely in his 1998 *Shakespeare: The Invention of the Human:* "When we first encounter him, Hamlet is a university student who is not being permitted to return to his studies. He does not ap pear to be more than twenty years old, yet in Act V he is revealed to be at least thirty, after a passage of a few weeks at most. And yet none of this mat ters: he is always both the youngest and the oldest personality in the drama."

Put aside Professor Bloom's faulty calendar arithmetic. (The action encompasses four months, as explained below and detailed in Chapter Two.) "None of this matters"? If not, then for discussions of *Hamlet*, nothing matters. (This is arguably the case, especially if you adopt Hamlet's "the rest is silence" existentialism. But like the existentialists, I choose to pretend that this stuff is actually important.) Just saying that Hamlet is "both the youngest and the oldest personality" is…less than satisfying.

So I had to go looking for the answer myself. And I found it. Hamlet is a teen.

Sixeteene Years Had Hamlet the Dane

At this point most of you are scrambling for your *Arden* or your *Riverside,* to Act 5, Scene 1, the graveyard scene. "It's right there!" you're sputtering. "It says he's thirty!"

And it's true; in the accepted, edited texts that almost everyone reads, the gravedigger says that he started as sexton (gravedigger, bell-ringer, church cleaner) the day that young Hamlet was born, and that he's "been sexton here, man and boy, thirty years." 5.1.69 And not fifteen lines later, the gravedigger says of Yorick, "Here's a skull now hath lien you i' th' earth three and twenty years." 5.1.73 If Hamlet rode on Yorick's shoulders and kissed his lips at age four or seven, Hamlet is 27 or 30. These oddly obtrusive items, plus two others discussed below, seem to bend over backwards to set Hamlet's age at thirty.

But I just plain knew this was wrong. The play doesn't make sense if Hamlet is thirty. So I went back to my *Riverside,* and in the textual notes I discovered what I'd halfway expected. The earliest published version of

Hamlet (the First Quarto, a.k.a. "Q1," published in 1603) omits the gravedigger's 30-year statement entirely, and has Yorick in the ground only 12
years instead of 23 Q1:3361—making Hamlet 16 or 20. G. Blakemore Evans,
the *Riverside's* textual editor, adds the unembellished comment, "Q1 thus
makes Hamlet a very young man."

The First Quarto

But how reliable is the First Quarto of 1603? It's definitely one of the "bad"
quartos; it's half the length of the Second Quarto (1604) and First Folio
(1623). (Scholars disagree on which of these is the most authoritative.) And
what's left in Q1 is in many cases a travesty rather than a tragedy, probably
set down from memory by the actor who played Marcellus and perhaps
other roles, including Voltemand. ("To be, or not to be, I there's the
point,/To Die, to sleepe, is that all? I all:" Q1:1710 It just gets worse from
there.)

Given how badly many scenes are savaged in Q1, the tendency of editors
is to throw most of it out as garbage. (Many find interest in the stage directions, as presumed accounts of actual performances.) But there are hundreds
of lines that vary by only a word or spelling here, or a punctuation mark
there. If the text's from memory, it's from an actor's memory. And that actor—Shakespeare's fellow player and *Hamlet's* first editor—clearly thought
that Hamlet was a youth.

Q1 is a contemporaneous report from an active and memory-trained
participant in some of the earliest performances of *Hamlet*. It doesn't have
the authority of Shakespeare's pen, but it has a third-party authority on the
play's early presentations that the rewrite artist and his editors, proofreaders,
typesetters, and correctors can't claim. Professor Jenkins disagrees: "the only
conclusion to be drawn...is that the reporter had a poor memory for numbers." But given the additional evidence from the more authoritative texts
detailed here, that is not the only conclusion.

The First Folio

This discovery in Q1 led to another contradiction in the far more authoritative First Folio text. In F1, the gravedigger's line reads, "Why heere in Den-
marke: I have bin sixteene [*not* sexten] heere, man and Boy thirty yeares."
F1:3351 This "sixteene" is ignored or at best buried in the textual footnotes
in every modern edition. (This even in the editions that claim to take the

First Folio as their "copy text"; they all opt for the Second Quarto's "sexton" reading.)

The line is quite easily and reasonably parsed: "I have been gravedigger here for sixteen years, and I've been living here in Denmark man and boy for thirty." (Thanks to Christopher Gauntt for putting me on this track.) Replacing the comma with a dash in modern editions would make it quite clear for today's readers. (All modern-spelling editions make free with changes to punctuation in aid of clarity.)

> "Why here in Denmark. I have been sixeteene here—man and boy
> thirty years."

It's the gravedigger who's 30, not Hamlet. His apprenticeship in the trade started at the normal age for Elizabethans, about fourteen.

The only way to make the line read otherwise is to replace "sixeteene" with "sexton" (which is what somebody, at some point, seems to have done in Q2, which reads "sexten"). But "Sixeteene" is patently *not* a variant spelling of "sexton." Only 72 lines before F1's "sixteen," "Sextons Spade" F1:3279 is spelled quite correctly (though typically without the apostrophe). In *Much Ado*, where "sexton" appears more than a dozen times, neither the quarto nor folio versions include any variant like this. In a search of publications between 1590 and 1625 in Chadwyck-Healy's Literature Online (LION) full-text database of early modern texts, there's not a single instance of "sexton" spelled even vaguely like this one. Out of a couple of dozen (wildly) variant spellings for "sexton" cited in the *Oxford English Dictionary*, only one usage begins with "six"—this one. There are many usages of "sixeteene" in LION, though (see examples at princehamlet.com). They all mean "sixteen."

In Osric and Hamlet's wager count of Barbary horses and French rapiers in F1, "sixe" is used three times while "six" is used once. F1: 3616-3627 And Hamlet speaks to the First Player of "some dosen or sixeene lines." F1: 1581 The "e" seems to be entirely optional in F1. (Q1 and Q2 use "six..." throughout; Q2 speaks twice of a "sexten," while Q1 never mentions one.) "Sixeteene" was a quite common spelling in Shakespeare's day (though "sixteene" was by far the most common)

"Sixeteene" is a completely unheard-of spelling for "sexton"; in F1 it clearly means "sixteen." This is one instance where a simple and obvious reading has been buried in the "accepted" text by dozens of editors' (largely silent) emen-

dations over the centuries. But it can't just be ignored if we give F1 the author
ity it deserves. It says quite clearly that Hamlet is 16. (Though as I argue in
Chapter Two, I believe he turned seventeen during his sea voyage.)

Like Q2, F1 does have the 23-year Yorick line (F1 reads "three &
twenty"), not 12 years as in Q1. How can we account for that? I can only say
that given all the evidence in this chapter, Q1's 12-year reading is more
credible; it conforms with F1's "sixteene" and with everything else in the
play. How did it get changed to 23 in Q2 and F1? There have been many
possible (and diverse) speculations about the play's 20- or 30-year course of
emendation, editing, and publication, buttressed by mountains of scholarship, but none rises above the level of surmise and supposition. There's just
not enough evidence to know. (See Appendix A: A Tragicall Hystorie of
Hamlet's Age.)

Counting on the Gravedigger

Even the gravedigger puts the lie to his own thirty-year lines, in another of
his oddly obtrusive date statements. Immediately after the sexten/sixteene
line, Hamlet asks him, "How long will a man lie i' th' earth ere he rot?"
"Eight or nine year," answers the gravedigger (in all three versions). "A tanner will last you nine year." 5.1.70

Not thirty lines later, with Yorick's skull in hand, Hamlet comments that
his "gorge rises" and he asks Horatio if Alexander's skull was similar: "And
smelt so? pah!" 5.1.80, 84 If a buried corpse decays in nine years, would it reek
with the play's ubiquitous decay after 23? Hamlet is not complaining of the
smell of freshly dug earth here. (And Yorick was not a tanner, after
all—though one might suppose that his flagons of Renish could have had
preservative value.) Yorick can't have been in the ground more than a dozen
years. This little date-laden interchange is directly between the two lines
that, in the accepted text, so insistently set Hamlet's age at thirty. Something
rotten here.

Thirty Dozen Moons

To diverge for a moment from the graveyard: There are two other items in
the play that suggest Hamlet is thirty—the "Murder of Gonzago" play, and
an offhand comment by Gertrude in the swordfight scene.

Gonzago opens with the Player King's "Full thirty times hath Phoebus'
cart gone round/.../And thirty dozen moons.../About the world have times

twelve thirties been,/Since love our hearts and Hymen did our hands/Unite comutual in most sacred bands." 3.2.102

Since the Player King and Queen are clearly representations of Old Hamlet and Gertrude, this repetitive insistence on thirty years (plus thirty days) since their marriage is hard to ignore in light of the gravedigger's words. Østerberg and Jenkins have discounted it as mere formula-speak, but the insistence on thirty years is undeniably there, and you can't just ignore its obvious echo in the gravedigger's lines.

Like the gravedigger's thirty-year statements, though, this snippet doesn't appear in Q1. The Player King says, "Full fortie yeares are past, their date is gone,/Since happy time ioyn'd both our hearts as one." Q1:2023 This thirty-year parallel tastes of the many direct echoes that pepper the play; it's likely to have been composed or adjusted—by whom and when is unclear—with the gravedigger's 30-year lines in mind. (See Appendix C for the source and more on the implications of the "Thirty dozen moons" passage.)

The only other item that suggests Hamlet is beyond his youth—Gertrude's comment during the swordfight that Hamlet is "fat and scant of breath" 5.2.222—doesn't appear in Q1 or F1, and it just reeks of a rewrite for a huffing Burbage that would draw a laugh from the pit. It's also a grim echo, in this death scene, of Hamlet's "we fat all creatures else to fat us, and we fat ourselves for maggots." 4.3.26

Several scholars over the years, by the way, have suggested that Burbage's weight (which some have pegged rather exactly at 250 pounds) made the "fat and scant of breath" line a telling indicator. But on digging, I discovered that the only evidence those scholars had for Burbage's supposed corpulence was...this very line. It's a circular myth that keeps cropping up, but has no legs.

If all we had were the discrepancies between the two gravedigger's statements in the Q1 and F1/Q2 editions, it would be easy to attribute them to numerical error by the Q1 reporter. But of the four items in the text that set Hamlet's age at thirty—two by the gravedigger, one by the player king, and one by Gertrude—all are missing from or contradicted by Q1, the most telling ("I have been sexten/sixteene here") is contradicted by F1, and all are contradicted by the gravedigger himself.

There's one other mildly persuasive and interesting item supporting Q1's "heres a scull hath bin here this dozen yeare": many critics have suggested that Yorick is a subtle elegy to Richard Tarleton, the most famous of Elizabethan comic actors and a favorite jester to the queen. Tarleton died in September, 1588—twelve years before the first performances of Shakespeare's *Hamlet.*

Noble Dust of Alexander

Only two dozen lines after the gravedigger's thirty-year references, Hamlet conjures up some of the most haunting imagery of the scene: "Why may not imagination trace the noble dust of Alexander, till he find it stopping a bunghole?" 5.1.86 Alexander's name is repeated like an incantation, five times in a dozen lines. And a dozen lines later, Hamlet invokes "Imperious Caesar, dead and turn'd to clay...." 5.1.89

Consider: Alexander led his father's armies into battle at sixteen. He became king at nineteen, following his father's murder. (And by the time he died at age thirty-one, he had conquered the known world.) Caesar, likewise, was thrust into the machinations of power after his father's death, at age sixteen, and was leading men into battle at eighteen. (For more on Caesar *cum* Hamlet, see Chapters 2 and 5, on Hamlet and Caesar's times with pirates.)

Alexander's life was common Elizabethan fare, and London theatergoers had been treated to Shakespeare's *Julius Caesar* multiple times in the years preceding *Hamlet's* release. The parallel between young Hamlet and those warlike young sovereigns—lodged here in the scene that so consciously and repeatedly sets times, durations, and ages—is more than suggestive. Certainly the classics-battered Oxford and Cambridge denizens and graduates would have copped to it.

Fortinbras: The Delicate and Tender Prince

Speaking of young warriors, let's look to Fortinbras. We know—as we know most things, from the gravedigger—that young Hamlet was born on the day old Hamlet slew old Fortinbras in single combat. 5.1.57 Fortinbras must have been conceived before that day, or he'd be hard-pressed to claim his princehood. So he is at most nine months Hamlet's junior. Ignore Professor Bloom's reference to "the younger Fortinbras." If Hamlet's thirty, Fortinbras is thirty or older.

But of the eight times in the play that Fortinbras is mentioned by name, in four of them he is called "young Fortinbras." This of a prince whose namesake father died at least sixteen years ago. Of the four instances remaining, in one Fortinbras is referring to himself; in another he's just been called 'young Fortinbras'; and in a third, Hamlet is giving him his dying word of succession.

Fortinbras is still under his ailing uncle's thumb; he and his army are brought up with a round turn after Claudius's embassy to old Norway via Voltemand and Cornelius: "...he sent out to suppress/His nephew's levies...sends out arrests/On Fortinbras, which he, in brief, obeys,/Receives rebuke from Norway, and in fine,/Makes vow before his uncle…" 2.2.69

Even more telling, in his "How all occasions do inform against me" soliloquy, as Hamlet watches Fortinbras's scrounged-together army pass through Denmark, Hamlet refers to Fortinbras as "a delicate and tender prince." 4.4.53

Now consider that Hamlet is speaking of a roughshod, warlike young prince. Horatio tells us that Fortinbras, "Of unimproved mettle hot and full,/Hath in the skirts of Norway here and there/Shark'd up a list of lawless resolutes/For food and diet…" 1.1.113 He's leading twenty thousand troops to "gain a little patch of ground/That hath in it no profit but the name," 4.4.22 to "fight for a plot/Whereon the numbers cannot try the cause,/Which is not tomb enough and continent/To hide the slain." 4.4.67

If this warlike Fortinbras were 30, even 25, even 21—in full beard and strength of arms—would Hamlet describe him as "a delicate and tender prince"? Would Horatio speak of his "unimproved mettle"? This Hamlet (and Laertes) alter-ego, this brash young sovereign, brings Hal, Edward IV, and Essex to mind (and Alexander and Caesar), not Brutus or Henry IV. Fortinbras has got to be a teen. And if he's a teen, so is Hamlet.

The Morn and Liquid Dew of Youth

Fortinbras isn't the only one who's spoken of as a young man. Horatio, Laertes, Polonius, the ghost, all refer to Hamlet as a youth. Hamlet even does it himself. Here are the main examples:

Horatio to Bernardo and Marcellus	"Let us impart what we have seen tonight/Unto young Hamlet." 1.1.189
Laertes to Ophelia	"For Hamlet, and the trifling of his favor,/Hold it a fashion and a toy in blood,/A violet in the youth of primy nature;" 1.3.8
Polonius to Ophelia	"he is young" 1.3.132
Ghost to Hamlet	"I could a tale unfold whose lightest

	word/Would harrow up thy soul, freeze thy young blood," 1.5.21
	"but know, thou noble youth,/The serpent that did sting thy father's life,/Now wears his crown." 1.5.45
Claudius to Rosencrantz and Guilden-stern	"being of so young days brought up with him,/And sith so neighbour'd to his youth and havior," 2.2.13
Hamlet to Rosencrantz and Guilden-stern	"let me conjure you, by the rights of our fellowship, by the consonancy of our youth," 2.2.246
Claudius	"This mad young man" 4.1.22

Every reference to Hamlet in the play that refers to age casts him as a youth. And an elegy to Richard Burbage by Joseph Fletcher, circa 1619, does as well (and shows that Burbage did in fact pull off the personation of youth); it refers to Burbage's roles as "young Hamlet, old Heironymo…" Laertes, Ophelia, and Osric, Rosencrantz and Guildenstern, likewise, are repeatedly referred to as youths. (I won't bother you with all those citations, though they're easily compiled.)

Hamlet the Student

All these references to Hamlet's youth aren't surprising; we find out in his first scene that he's a student at Wittenberg, "intent in going back to school." 1.2.116 The student theme is a constant throughout the play—in Hamlet's relationship to Horatio, to his "schoolfellows" 3.4.224 Rosencrantz and Guild-enstern, to Laertes, even in his banter with the players.

If nothing else in the play convinced us, this in itself should make clear that Hamlet is a teen. The reference to Wittenberg is anachronistic—it was a center of learning in Shakespeare's time, not Hamlet's—but whichever pe-riod you're referring to, princes didn't go to school at age thirty. To choose one example of many: Henry Wriothesley, the flamboyant young Earl of Southampton, to whom Shakespeare dedicated *Venus and Adonis* and *Rape of Lucrece,* entered St. John's College, Cambridge, at age 12; he was finished with the sober drudgeries of university and carousing at court by age 17. That was an Elizabethan nobleman's normal pattern. A career more typical of our time, but still accelerated, was playwright Christopher Marlowe's (from the citizen or artisan class, not the aristocracy): he took his B. A. at age 20, and his M. A. at 23. I've compiled many other examples at princehamlet.com. In 400 years, no critic has given a reasonable explanation that I've found of why a 30-year-old Hamlet would still be a student.

J. W. Hales did take a stab at it in 1876, quoting Thomas Nashe's 1592 *Pierce Pennilesse*. In the course of vilifying the Danes, Pierce says, "For fashion sake some will put their children to schoole, but they set them not to it till they are foureteene yeere olde: so that you shall see a great boy with a beard learne his A B C. and sit weeping under the rod, when he is thirtie yeeres old." Given Pierce's disregard of fact throughout this screed, though (and Nashe's apparent ignorance of things Danish), this can hardly be taken as reliable historical report. Shakespeare was keenly aware of Nashe's works (the body of evidence is too extensive to detail here), so Pierce's extended calumny of the besotted Danes is perhaps the very passage that Hamlet complains of to Horatio: "This heavy-headed revel east and west/Makes us traduc'd and tax'd of other nations./They clip us drunkards, and with swinish phrase/Soil our addition." 1.4.21

How Many Years Hath Hamlet the Play?

Some critics have tried to explain the student discrepancy by suggesting that the duration of the play is thirteen years. But the text of the play makes this impossible. I explore all these references in detail in Chapter Two, but a summary is useful here. (See the graphical timeline.)

- When the play opens, Hamlet tells us that old Hamlet is "but two months dead." 1.2.142

- In the mousetrap scene, Ophelia says old Hamlet has been dead "twice two months." 3.2.83 So two months have passed. Hamlet leaves immediately for England (after excoriating his mother and disposing of Polonius).

- When Claudius is conscripting Laertes into his plot to kill Hamlet, he says that Lamord, a gentleman of Normandy, had spoken highly of Laertes' swordsmanship "in Hamlet's hearing…two months since." 4.7.79, 89 (This one's easy to miss; the two ends of this statement are ten lines apart!) So Hamlet has been gone on his sea voyage less than two months when he returns in the very next (graveyard) scene—at most six

months after his father's death, four months from the beginning of the
play.

• Multiple references in the text (detailed in Chapter Two) show that it's
  less than a day between Hamlet's return in the graveyard scene and the
  swordfight.

So the action spans four months at most. Hamlet has developed in those
four months, but he sure hasn't turned thirty.

Amleth and the Ur-Hamlet

Given that Shakespeare lifted the basic plot of his play from earlier sources
(as T. S. Eliot said, "Immature poets imitate; mature poets steal"), it's worth
looking at those sources to see how old the prince is.

Shakespeare's main source, directly or indirectly, was the Amleth story in
F. de Belleforest's five-volume French publication, *Le Cinquiesme Tome des
Histoires Tragique*, published in France in various editions between 1570 and
1582. That story was in turn borrowed from the Danish historian Saxo
Grammaticus's Latin *Gesta Danorum*, written circa 1200 and published in
1514. Belleforest's version speaks of the uncle's concern that if Amleth "once
attained to man's estate, he would not long delay the time to revenge the
death of his father." (This is actually from an anonymous English translation
of Belleforest's version, published in London in 1608—eight years after
Hamlet debuted—but perhaps circulating in manuscript or a lost earlier edition prior to that.)

So in Belleforest, the prince is not a man yet. But there is a good chance
that Shakespeare did not have (or could not read) Belleforest's French version—that he took the story from an earlier and now lost play which scholars call the *Ur-Hamlet,* that we first hear mention of in 1589, usually
attributed to playwright Thomas Kyd. Notably, Kyd was fluent in French—he
translated Garnier's *Cornelia* in 1594—so could have read Belleforest. By all
appearances Shakespeare had little or no French; his plays include multiple
scenes making fun of characters' mangling of that language (the scenes with
Henry and the French princess Catherine in *Henry V*—in which she man-
gles English in return and uses only schoolgirl French—being perhaps the
most amusing). We know from contemporary references that this early

Hamlet was played by Shakespeare's company and perhaps others between 1589 and 1594, and perhaps in late 1599/early 1600.

It's possible that the *Ur-Hamlet* playwright changed the hero's age from Belleforest's pre-adult to 30, and that Shakespeare adopted that when he wrote his play, but there's no reason to think that happened. And I personally tend to side with Harold Bloom and Peter Alexander in believing the *Ur-Hamlet* to be Shakespeare's own early attempt at *Hamlet* (perhaps co-authored with Kyd), brought to fruition a decade later—in which case we're back with Belleforest as Shakespeare's source.

And in Belleforest, the prince has not "attained to man's estate."

The Question of Character

So there's all sorts of evidence in and surrounding the play showing that Hamlet is a teen. But beyond all this "hard" evidence, there's Hamlet's character. In addition to being brilliant, noble, acceptably eloquent, and all those other things we love about him, at least until the final act he's naïve ("meet it is I set it down/That one may smile, and smile, and be a villain!" 1.5.115), peevish, petulant, wildly changeable from moment to moment, maddeningly and intransigently judgmental, a know-it-all theater critic, and a shallow philosopher who actually believes he can solve the eternal human problems that nobody else has succeeded at. If that's not a teenager, what is?

And if Hamlet's a teen, many other mysteries in the play come clear—from big questions of character and motivation to some seemingly intractable quibbles and puns. That's where I go in Chapters Three through Five—to the implications of Hamlet's youth.

But before I get to that, in Chapter Two I track down the dozens of date and time references that are embedded throughout the play. Because there's new matter there—more than I ever thought possible to find in this oh-so-discovered country.

CHAPTER TWO

Abstract and Brief
Chronicles of the Time

A scholarly version of this chapter ("Hamlet as The Christmas Prince: Certain Speculations on Hamlet, the Calendar, Revels, and Misrule") is available online in Volume 7.3 of Early Modern Literary Studies.

While I was sorting through all the evidence about Hamlet's age, I was constantly struck by the number of references in the play to times, days, dates, and durations. Time is right up there with decay and mortality in any list of the play's obsessions. (This is true throughout Shakespeare's plays and poems, most especially in the sonnets; Donald Foster, for instance, has spoken of Shakespeare's "nearly obsessive concern with man's relation to time.") My immediate question was, "Why?" What purpose do all these references serve? This being *Hamlet,* the implications are manifold; they weave their way throughout the fabric of the play.

But before exploring those implications, I started to map out all the references. (See the graphical timeline.) As Harley Granville-Barker explains in his 1936 preface to *Hamlet,* the action of the play is broken into three main "movements," or sequences of events. For ease of reference, I've given a name to each sequence. (Note that these sequences encompass both depicted and reported events.)

- **The ghost sequence.** The ghost's appearances, the opening court scene, and Laertes' and Polonius' talks with Ophelia.

- **The mousetrap sequence.** Beginning with Hamlet's (reported) appearance in Ophelia's closet, spanning the get-thee-to-a-nunnery scene, mousetrap play, and Gertrude's closet, and ending with Hamlet's encounter with Fortinbras' army and departure for England.

- **The gravedigger sequence.** Beginning with Ophelia's madness, spanning the graveyard scene and the "interim," and ending with the swordfight.

There's a five-scene beginning, a ten-scene middle, and a five-scene end. Shakespeare probably didn't identify scenes explicitly—there are none specified in the *Hamlet* quartos, and only a handful in Acts One and Two in the Folio. But a certain structure and symmetry is apparent nevertheless.

While this description and Granville-Barker's discussion of *Hamlet*'s "time structure" do much to clarify the progression and intervals of the play (and suggest that it should be presented with two intermissions), obsessions being what they are, I started tallying all the references to days and times—including many that Granville-Barker failed to note. And happily, obsessions have their rewards. I found in the text a remarkably detailed chronology of the events in *Hamlet*—in many cases specified down to the day or hour. The coherence of that chronology only breaks down at the end of the play—and then only partially.

The chronology doesn't march in complete lockstep, of course; Shakespeare used timing and sequence for various and nefarious narrative, dramatic, and theatrical purposes, and sometimes uncertainty best served those turns. Many have noticed the "telescoping" of time in the ramparts scenes, for instance, which go from midnight to dawn quite rapidly, and the conspicuous uncertainty about whether it's midnight or one. And there are various troublesome items to do with Horatio: he seems to have been at Elsinore for a month or two, for instance—since King Hamlet's funeral—before he sees his friend Hamlet for the first time. But even given those items, it's impossible to ignore the ubiquitous, insistent, and coherent references to times and dates in the play.

Both A. C. Bradley and Steve Sohmer have explored this chronology in their works, but Bradley's analysis is incomplete, and Sohmer's—while it starts with the discovery that I discuss next—proceeds to crack on the rocks of some tenuous assertions.

The Ghost Walks

The biggest breakthrough for me in sorting out all the date and time references was not actually mine. Steve Sohmer has demonstrated in his "Certain Speculations on Hamlet, the Calendar, and Martin Luther" in *Early Modern Literary Studies* that the ghost first walked on four nights of Friday, October 30 through Monday, November 2, 1601. It seems impossible that the play could contain evidence supporting that precise dating, but Sohmer is quite convincing, and his work led me to several discoveries that make the whole edifice of evidence pretty compelling.

Following is a summary of Sohmer's key points, with my commentary in square brackets pointing out some additional evidence, and some difficulties with his analysis.

- The composition of Shakespeare's *Hamlet* has been dated to 1600 or (more likely) 1601. [See Appendix A for further discussion of this dating.]

- Shakespeare and other Elizabethan poets often used the liturgical calendar as a structural device. The holy days were pervasive for Elizabethans. "Correspondence, contracts, leases, liens, and tenancies—all were dated with reference to the church calendar." [See Appendix D for more insights on the importance of calendars and almanacs to Shakespeare and Elizabethans in general—especially Elizabethan poets.]

- References in the text [laid out in the table below] tell us that the ghost appeared on four successive nights.

- The sentinels' difficulty seeing each other in the opening scene—calling out repeatedly for identification—suggests a dark, moonless night. [It can't be cloudy, because Bernardo refers to "yond same star that's westward from the pole," 1.1.48 and Horatio speaks of a red sunrise: "the morn in russet mantle clad/Walks o'er the dew of yon high eastward hill." 1.1.186 But, see my comments below on an error in Sohmer's calculations here.]

- Francisco tells us, " 'Tis bitter cold." 1.1.10 Hamlet echoes that the next night: "The air bites shrowdly, it is very cold." 1.4.3

- Marcellus comments on "that season.../Wherein our Savior's birth is celebrated,/.../...no spirit dare stir abroad,/.../No fairy takes, nor witch hath power to charm,/So hallowed, and so gracious, is that time." 1.1.178 Sohmer identifies this with Advent—November 27th to December 25 in 1601. [The first Sunday of Advent was actually November 29.] The Ghost could not walk during this period.

So the encounters with the ghost occur in winter, before November 29 or after December 25.

- The star Deneb, which Sohmer identifies as Bernardo's star, lay "westward from the pole, circa 1:00 a.m. during the period 30 October–10 November, 1601." [See Appendix E for other possibilities for this star.]

- "2 November 1601 was a moonless night, both in London and at Elsinore."

There is an unfortunate miscalculation here. Sohmer cites the moon's position according the now-current Gregorian calendar, not the Julian calendar of sixteenth-century England and Denmark, which was offset by ten days (see Appendix D). By the Julian calendar, the moon on Halloween, October 31, 1601, was full—with all the spooky connotations that still attach.

In fact, while Bernardo stands on the ramparts looking north toward Polaris at 1 am on November 2, the almost-full moon is almost directly behind him in the south, sixty degrees above the horizon. This makes sense given Hamlet's "What may this mean,/That thou, dead corse, again in complete steel/Revisits thus the glimpses of the moon." 1.4.51 It's probably most accurate to imagine a night of scudding, broken clouds, with the full moon glimpsed, then hidden, then revealed again.

This may seem to dash Sohmer's theory, but there are other obvious ways to explain the sentries' inability to see each other—from broken clouds to various methods of staging and blocking. With a full moon, this could make for some pretty stagey staging.

- The four days October 30 to November 2, 1601 were, respectively, the Feast of Marcellus [!], All Hallows Eve, All Saint's Day, and All Soul's Day. It was a common Elizabethan belief that spirits walked the night on All

Hallows Eve. The last three of these holidays were all about remembrance of the dead. [Saint Marcellus, remembered on October 30, was a Roman centurion, an officer or captain, who was executed for his refusal to participate in the revels celebrating the emperor's birthday.]

All Hallow's Eve. All Souls Day. All Saint's Day. Together, Hallowmas. I could not but remember the ghost's final injunction, echoed by Hamlet—"Remember me"—and the play's constant and insistent remembrance of the dead, and of things past.

The following table may be helpful in sorting out all the "yesternights" and "tonights" referencing the ghost's appearances, and their correlation to Sohmer's proposed dates. It also highlights how fastidiously, often repetitively, the times and days are catalogued in the play.

Day/Date	Time/Event	Text References
Friday, Oct. 30, Feast of Marcellus To Saturday morning, Oct. 31 Saturday, Oct. 31, All Hallows Eve To Sunday morning, Nov. 1	Between midnight and 1 a.m. (reported). Ghost appears twice to Bernardo and Marcellus.	Marcellus: "…this dreaded sight twice seen of us;" 1.1.35 Bernardo to Horatio: "…let us once again assail your ears,/…./What we have two nights seen./…./Last night of all,/When yond same star…/…./Where now it burns,…/The bell then beating one—" [cut off by the ghost's appearance] 1.1.42 Marcellus: "Thus twice before, and jump at this dead hour,/…hath he gone by our watch." 1.1.81 Horatio: "My lord, I think I saw him yesternight./…/Two nights together had these gentlemen,/…/Been thus encount'red:…/And I with them the third night kept the watch," 1.2.196, 205, 217
Sunday, Nov. 1, All Saints' Day To Monday morning, Nov. 2	Midnight: Bernardo and Marcellus tell Horatio (again) of ghost's appearance on the preceding two nights. Ghost appears to Bernardo, Marcellus, and Horatio.	Francisco: "You come most carefully upon your hour." Bernardo: "'Tis now strook twelf." 1.1.8 Marcellus, on agreeing to inform Hamlet: "I this morning know/Where we shall find him most convenient." 1.1.194

Monday, Nov. 2 All Souls' Day To Tuesday morning, Nov. 3	Evening: Horatio, Marcellus, and Bernardo tell Hamlet of the preceding three nights.	Hamlet to Bernardo: "Good even, sir." 1.2.173 Apparently Hamlet is engaged in the opening court scene, so Horatio, Marcellus, and Bernardo don't connect with him until evening.
	Just before midnight: Ghost appears to Marcellus, Horatio, and Hamlet.	Hamlet: "Stayed it long?" Horatio: "While one with moderate haste might tell a hundreth." Bernardo and Marcellus: "Longer, longer." Horatio: "Not when I saw't." 1.2.253
		Hamlet: "Hold you the watch tonight?/.../I will watch to-night,/.../Upon the platform 'twixt aleven and twelf/I'll visit you." 1.2.237, 260, 271
		Hamlet: "What hour now?" Horatio: "I think it lacks of twelf." Marcellus: "No, it is stroock." Horatio: "Indeed? I heard it not. It then draws near the season/Wherein the spirit held his wont to walk." 1.4.5

The night of October 31/November 1 had for centuries been celebrated as Celtic New Year; even in pre-Christian times it was believed that disruptive spirits roamed on that night. And it was also, at least from medieval times, a night of costumes, masks, revels, inversion of roles, real and play-acted rebellion, and…theatrical productions.

All Hallows was also a time for election of "mock kings," "lords of revels," or "kings of misrule." These lords would reign over the revels season through Christmas and Twelfth Night (January 5, another night of inversion and mock rebellion), often ending their reigns at Shrovetide (which had— and still has—perhaps the greatest association with carnival and misrule). As it turns out, these festivals of misrule figure in the later movements of the play as well.

Religious holidays started at sunset the night preceding the holiday; that night was called the "vigil." So Friday night/Saturday morning, when the ghost first appeared, was the vigil of All Hallows Eve.

Another point Sohmer brings up, but doesn't address to my complete satisfaction: the discussion of the time at which Hamlet, Horatio, and Marcellus arrive on the ramparts (Horatio: "…it lacks of twelf," 1.4.6 and Marcellus: "No, it is stroock.") Sohmer explains: "Hamlet has said he would arrive on the platform ''twixt aleven and twelf.' Given his eagerness to see the Ghost, it's hard to believe he would arrive behind his time. In order to make its fourth appearance on All Souls' Day, the Ghost would have to appear before midnight."

But that doesn't explain the seemingly intentional contradiction here. Is it before or after midnight? Time is definitely distorted, compressed, in this scene and in the second ramparts scene as well. It goes from midnight through one o'clock to dawn in 130 lines (in Denmark, in the winter). But that doesn't explain the contradiction.

In perusing the First Quarto, I found a difference that perhaps clarifies the question. Comparing the versions:

F1/Q2 F1: 607; Q2: 607
*Hora.*I thinke it lackes of twelfe.
Mar. No, it is strooke.
Hora. Indeede; I heard it not, it then drawes neere the season,
Wherein the spirit held his wont to walke   *A florish of trumpets*
What does this meane my Lord?   *and 2. peeces goes of.*
   (The stage direction is in Q2 only, not F1.)

Q1 Q1: 607
Hor. I think it lackes of twelue,   *Sound Trumpets.*
Mar. No, t'is strucke.
Hor. Indeed I heard it not, what doth this mean my lord?

In Q1, Marcellus mistakes the trumpet blare that "brays out" Claudius' draining of his draught of Rhenish for the striking of midnight. Nervous and edgy, he jumps at the sound, and replies too quickly. If this is correct, Sohmer is also correct that the ghost appears before midnight, hence on All Souls' Day—the day when all dead souls are remembered. Q1 is presumably from the memory of the actor who played Marcellus, so its stage directions here carry some authority.

Some of Sohmer's arguments regarding *Hamlet*'s relation to Martin Luther and the reformation are more difficult to accept. There are certainly relationships and echoes there. But some of Sohmer's calendrical relationships are dubious. In particular, he cites Corpus Christi (June 2–3) as the date of the swordfight, which is impossible to reconcile with the text. The action ends two months after the mousetrap at latest, four months after the opening scenes—by the first week of March.

Murder Most Foul

If we take Sohmer's dates for the Ghost's appearance as correct, at least provisionally, then based on Hamlet's "But two months dead, nay, not so much, not two" 1.2.142 on November 2, old Hamlet was murdered sometime shortly after September 2, 1601. The first week of September is about the latest it could have occurred, because the ghost says it was "Sleeping within my orchard,/My custom always of the afternoon". 1.5.67 After that date it would have been getting too cold for naps *al fresco.* (*Viz,* the improbable snowy winter nap scene that Branagh depicts in his film version.)

Sohmer, through some serpentine calculations, cites October 2 as the date of the murder, which directly contradicts Hamlet's "But two months dead." In *Shakespeare's Mystery Play* (p. 231) he explains that "Hamlet is confused about how long his father has been dead because he has recently journeyed from Wittenberg, where the calendar is Julian, to a place where the calendar is Gregorian." Even if that confusion was plausible, 1) both Wittenberg and Denmark were on the Julian calendar in Shakespeare's day (England until 1752), and 2) the discrepancy between the two calendars would only account for ten days, not a full month.

So I went looking for liturgical holidays in the first week of September, and found little. But then I remembered to look through the wonderfully organized and complete year-by-year history in Appendix C of the *Riverside.* And that's where I discovered the date that stopped me dead:

John Shakespeare—Will's father—was buried on September 8, 1601.

If we correlate King Hamlet's murder with John Shakespeare's death, that puts the date at Sunday, September 6 or Monday, September 7—a day or two before John Shakespeare's burial. This strongly supports Sohmer's opinion, shared by Dover Wilson and many others, that Shakespeare completed revisions of the *Hamlet* as we know it after September 1601. (See Appendix A for more discussion of *Hamlet's* textual history.)

The connection between the date of King Hamlet's murder and John Shakespeare's, for me at least, is remarkably moving. And it's even more so if we accept Nicholas Rowe's third- or fourth-hand report (reported almost a century after Shakespeare's death) that Shakespeare's greatest role was as the ghost:

...tho' I have inquir'd, I could never meet with any further Account of him this way, than that the top of his Performance was the Ghost in his own *Hamlet.* —From the introduction and Shakespeare biography in Rowe's 1709 edition of the plays.

By this account, Shakespeare played the role of King Hamlet's ghost, a father who "died" on the same day as Will's father, only two months before. And we hear in the ghost's words an alluringly close echo from the first paragraph of John Shakespeare's "Spiritual Last Will and Testament" (discovered—at least in part—in the rafter's of John Shakespeare's house 150 years after his death; see princehamlet.com for a transcript, discussion, and links). The testament reads (italics added):

"I may be possibly *cut off in the blossom of my sins,* and called to *render an account of all my transgressions* externally and internally, and that I may be *unprepared for the dreadful trial either by sacrament, penance, fasting, or prayer, or any other purgation* whatever..."

Compare the ghost's words: 1.5.84

Cut off even in the blossoms of my sin,
Unhousel'd, disappointed, unanel'd,
No reckoning made, but *sent to my account*
With all my imperfections on my head:
O, horrible! O, horrible! most horrible!

Word-for-word lifts from outside documents are extremely rare in Shakespeare, even with such seeming commonplaces as "blossom of my sins" and "render an account." (Shakespeare was much for commonplaces, but like Bottom in *Midsummer Night's Dream,* they are transformed.) And "blossom(s) of my sin(s)" is not a commonplace; my searches reveal no similar usages in any Elizabethan literature.

This singularity makes it seem likely that when composing these lines— whenever he composed them—Shakespeare had his father in mind. What scholarly consensus exists puts the date of John Shakespeare's testament around 1580. It seems unlikely it would have come to Shakespeare's mind twenty years later without some prompting; a "reading" of the will upon his father's death might well have provided that prompt.

This testament business may be spurious. The first couple of "articles" in the testament are of more questionable provenance and authenticity. (There was the issue of a missing first manuscript page, which later emerged...) A more likely explanation may be that the echo is there because the man who brought this document to light, John Jordan, fabricated those first articles out of broadcloth. The man probably knew his *Hamlet.* But the evidence for the burial dates remains.

O'erhasty Wedding

We know from Hamlet's "A little month, or ere those shoes were old/With which she followed my poor father's body,/.../...Within a month,/.../She married" 1.2.151 that Claudius and Gertrude's wedding happened within a month of old Hamlet's death—it sounds like just under a month. So the wedding would have occurred sometime in the first week of October. There were periods (Advent, for example) in which weddings were not allowed by the church without special license. (These licenses were generally available for nothing more than a fee and the trouble of attaining them; Shakespeare himself went to that trouble and expense for his marriage to Anne Hathaway, probably because she was pregnant at the time). The first week of October did not fall in any of those prohibited periods.

It's unclear when Claudius was crowned king. It must have been after the marriage (that's how these things are done). But whether it was "hard upon" 1.2.185 or as Dover Wilson surmises, just before the opening court scene, or sometime in between, on this the text is silent.

Christmas Break

The next question I tackled: how much time passes between the ghost sequence and the mousetrap sequence? This led to another revelation. It may be helpful to refer to the table below while reading the following points.

Ophelia's "Twice two months." In the mousetrap scene, Ophelia says King Hamlet has been dead "twice two months." 3.2.83 If he died in the first week of September 1601, the mousetrap sequence occurs in the first week of January, 1602. (This interchange, where Hamlet says, "my father died within's two hours," is one of Shakespeare's better plays on real time versus theater time—the mousetrap scene is about two hours into the play. Thanks to Steve Sohmer and his friend M. A. McGrail for noticing this fact.)

Rosencrantz and Guildenstern. It's not clear when the summons was sent to them, or where they were at the time. Claudius' mention that they are "of so young days brought up with him [Hamlet]" 2.2.13 tells us that they're probably Danish friends of Hamlet's, and Rosencrantz's comment to Gertrude and Claudius ("...the sovereign power you have of us," 2.2.30) supports their Danish citizenship. They seem to have arrived from outside the country, though, because Hamlet asks them what they've done that they should be sent to Denmark 2.2.226. They're referred to as "schoolfellows," 3.4.224 so it's quite likely they were at Wittenberg (their namesakes appear in the university rosters in the 1500s), but they could have been pre-university schoolfellows. See also Peter Usher's insights into the Rosencrantz and Guildenstern connection in Appendix D.

Claudius refers to "our hasty sending" for them in their first interview. 2.2.6 And based on Gertrude's reference to her "too much changed son" 2.2.40, it seems that they were summoned after Hamlet put his antic disposition on (November 2). There needs to have been time for them to receive the summons and then journey to Elsinore.

Voltemand and Cornelius. These ambassadors took ship for Norway immediately after the court scene, on November 2. (Claudius, when dispatching them, says, "Let your haste commend your duty." 1.2.41) They report to Claudius on their return 2.2.69:

> Upon our first, he sent out to suppress
> His nephew's levies, which to him appear'd
> To be a preparation 'gains't the Polack;
> But better looked into, he truly found
> It was against your Highness. Whereat griev'd,
> That so his sickness, age, and impotence
> Was falsely borne in hand, sends out arrests
> On Fortinbras, which he, in brief, obeys,
> Receives rebuke from Norway, and in fine,
> Makes vow before his uncle never more
> To give th' assay of arms against your Majesty.

So in the time since Voltemand and Cornelius departed, they traveled to Norway and met with the king. Norway sent messages to suppress Fortinbras' levying of troops, and looked into what those troops were being used for. On discovering that they were threatening Denmark, he sent for Fortinbras, who returned and made "vow before his uncle." Cornelius and Voltemand then returned to Denmark.

Two months seems a reasonable amount of time for these events to have occurred.

Hamlet's letters to Ophelia. On November 2, Polonius tells Ophelia to reject Hamlet's letters and other approaches. In reporting Hamlet's appearance in her closet, Ophelia reports that she has done so: "...as you did command/I did repel his letters, and denied/His access to me." 2.1.120

Polonius reports in more detail to Gertrude and Claudius. He gives them Hamlet's love letter, and continues 2.2.132:

> This in obedience hath my daughter shown me,
> And more above, hath his solicitings,
> As they fell out by time, by means, and place,
> All given to mine ear.

He then describes the course of events beginning with his warning her off on November 2: 2.2.151

> ...I prescripts gave her,
> That she should lock herself from his resort,
> Admit no messengers, receive no tokens.
> Which done, she took the fruits of my advice;
> And he repell'd, a short tale to make,
> Fell into a sadness, then into a fast,
> Thence to a watch, thence into a weakness,
> Thence into a lightness, and by this declension,
> Into the madness wherein now he raves,

So Hamlet has sent multiple letters to Ophelia without requite prior to his appearance in her closet, and the "declension" which Polonius describes in "a short tale" occurred over some period. (It makes no difference here that his description is perhaps fatuous; the duration's the thing.) Two months seems right.

Reynaldo's mission to Paris. In the opening line of Polonius' interview with Reynaldo, in which he sends him off to Laertes in Paris, he says, "Give him this money and these notes." 2.1.3 Laertes presumably took money with him when he departed on November 2, so some time must have passed that he's in need of another installment.

Ophelia's "twice two months" probably suffices to set the timing of this series of scenes in the first week of January, but the supporting evidence from all these other matters is interesting in that it shows the coherence of the chronology. (This new year's timing could explain at least one joke in the mousetrap, Hamlet's carping comment on the prologue: "Is this a prologue, or the posy of a ring?" 3.2.152 George Puttenham, in his widely influential *The Arte of English Poesie* of 1585, describes "posies" as "epigrammes that were sent usually for new yeares giftes…we do use them as devices in rings and armes and about such courtly purposes.")

Hamlet's "Monday Morning"

There's one other clue to the date of the mousetrap sequence—a flagrant one, from Hamlet in one of his flagrant moods. It's one of those toss-offs that's so frustrating to those of us who rely on the footnotes in the Riverside, Oxford, and Norton editions, et al.—frustrating because there is no footnote. None of the editors seems to know what it means. (Jenkins in his 1982 Arden notes does attempt an uncharacteristically lame explanation.)

After Rosencrantz tells Hamlet of the players' arrival, Polonius enters to tell Hamlet the same thing, which Hamlet makes mock of: "I will prophesy, he comes to tell me of the players, mark it. You say right, sir, a' Monday morning, 'twas then indeed." 2.2.277 To paraphrase: "Watch: I'll say what he's going to say before he says it." Then to Polonius, "If you're going to tell me the players arrived on Monday morning, you're right!"

So it's Monday morning in the first week of January, 1602. The players arrive on January 4.

Wednesday, January 6 was Epiphany, also known as Twelfth Day. The night of January 5—the night the mousetrap was played—was Twelfth Night.

This makes all sorts of sense. Like All Hallow's Eve, Twelfth Night was a night of revels, performances, masking, costumes, and misrule. It was the culminating event of the Christmas revels season at court. Every year between 1582 and 1608, save two, there was a performance at court on Epiphany (and four different companies played on Epiphany in 1601). During the seven years 1596 to 1602, four of the Epiphany performances were by Shakespeare's company (including 1601, but not including 1602).

There's a further significance, though, to this date in *Hamlet*. The Christmas season, with its worship, observances, solemnities, and inhibitions, ends at sunset on Twelfth Night. And on that very night, at "the very witching time of night,/When churchyards yawn and hell itself breathes out/Contagion to this world," 3.2.277 the ghost walks again.

Recall Marcellus' somewhat odd reference, to "that season…/Wherein our Savior's birth is celebrated,/…/…no spirit dare stir abroad,/…/No fairy takes, nor witch hath power to charm,/So hallowed, and so gracious, is that time." 1.1.178 It clearly refers not just to Advent, as Sohmer suggests, but to the twelve days of Christmas as well. As soon as that proscribed holy season ends, just after midnight, the ghost walks again.

The Mousetrap Sequence

So the play tells us exactly when the mousetrap sequence happens. It also tells us that the mousetrap events occur over four days, and on which days the events occur. Again, a table of days and references may help to sort it all out. All the scenes are included, but the events are condensed, including only those that have bearing on the chronology of the mousetrap sequence.

Act and Scene	Event	Text References
Monday, January 4		
Reported by Ophelia to Polonius (2.1)	Hamlet appears in Ophelia's closet.	2.1.84
2.1	Polonius' interview with Reynaldo	Reynaldo's exit immediately precedes Ophelia's entrance.

		Ophelia tells Polonius of Hamlet's visit.	Ophelia: "Oh my lord, my lord, I have been so affrighted!" 2.1.85
			Polonius: "Come, go with me. I will go seek the King./...Come, go we to the King./.../Come." 2.1.113, 130, 133
2.2		Cornelius and Voltemand report on their embassy.	Claudius: "...at our more considered time we'll read,/Answer, and think upon this business." 2.2.90
		Polonius tells Gertrude and Claudius of Hamlet's visit to Ophelia's closet.	2.2.117
		Hamlet's encounter with the Players	Hamlet: "...we'll hear a play tomorrow./..../We'll ha't to-morrow night." 2.2.375, 377

Tuesday, January 5: Twelfth Night (and morning of January 6, Epiphany)

3.1		Rosencrantz, Guildenstern, and Polonius report on Hamlet to Claudius and Gertrude; Polonius invites them to the play.	Rosencrantz of Hamlet and the players: "...they have already order/This night to play before him." 3.1.24
		Nunnery scene	Claudius: "I have in quick determination/Thus set it down: he shall with speed to England" 3.1.151
			Polonius: "...after the play/Let his queen-mother all alone entreat him..." 3.1.164
3.2		Mousetrap	
		Hamlet summoned to Gertrude	Hamlet: "'Tis now the very witching time of night,/When churchyards yawn and hell itself breathes out/Contagion to this world." 3.2.277
3.3		Claudius' "repentance"	Claudius to Rosencrantz and Guildenstern: "I your commission will forthwith dispatch,/And he to England shall along with you./The terms of our estate may not endure/Hazard so near 's as doth hourly grow/Out of his brows." 3.3.5
3.4		Gertrude's closet; the ghost walks.	

4.1	Gertrude reports to Claudius.	Claudius: "The sun no sooner shall the mountains touch/But we will ship him hence." 4.1.32
4.2	Rosencrantz and Guildenstern ask Hamlet for the body.	
4.3	Claudius sends Hamlet to England.	Claudius: "...must send thee hence/With fiery quickness; therefore prepare thyself,/The bark is ready, and the wind at help,/Th' associates tend, and every thing is bent/For England." 4.3.38 "Follow him at foot, tempt him with speed aboard./Delay it not, I'll have him hence to-night./Away, for every thing is seal'd and done/That else leans on th' affair. Pray you make haste." 4.3.49

Wednesday, January 6: Epiphany		
4.4	Day: Hamlet encounters Fortinbras' army headed for the Polack wars.	
Reported in letter from Hamlet to Horatio in 4.6	Night: Hamlet exchanges Rosencrantz and Guildenstern's packet.	"Ere we were two days old at sea, a pirate of very warlike appointment gave us chase...." 4.6.12

Thursday, January 7		
Reported by Hamlet to Horatio in 5.2	Hamlet taken by pirates.	Hamlet telling of his packet switching: "Now the next day/Was our sea-fight," 5.2.59

The mousetrap is played the night after the players arrive, Hamlet takes ship the next morning, and the following day he's taken by the pirates. While the explicit references to chronology here are pretty tight, there are a couple of less-than-ironclad areas having to do with Ophelia and Fortinbras.

Ophelia's Closet

There's a possible delay between Hamlet's appearance in Ophelia's closet, her report to Polonius, and his report to Claudius. But it seems pretty clear that they happen close upon each other. When Ophelia enters with her "Oh my lord my lord, I have been so affrighted!", 2.1.85 and Polonius responds with his repeated urgings to hasten to the king, it's clear that she has just encountered Hamlet, and that Polonius is intent on going directly to Claudius, which he does in the next scene. (In Q1 she accompanies him to see the king, but in Q2 and F1, Polonius presumably pauses to get her full account and Hamlet's love letter; he then reports them himself *sans* Ophelia.)

It's in that ensuing scene that Hamlet makes his reference to Monday morning, and says they'll have the play the next night.

Ophelia's Many a Day

Another problematic bit is Ophelia's opening line to Hamlet in the nunnery scene: "How does your lord this many a day?" (III.i.91). If she saw him in her closet only the day before, it seems odd. But then consider that Hamlet didn't even speak to her in that encounter:

Polonius: What said he?

Ophelia: He took me by the wrist, and held me hard...

She proceeds to describe his alarming actions, but he never says a word. So when she asks how he's been doing all this time, it makes sense given that her only encounter with him in the last two months was this silent and unnerving one the day before.

Fortinbras' Promised March

There's another curious issue of timing in Hamlet's encounter with Fortinbras' army. It makes sense that the army should be on this march on this day, following a respite during Christmas so the levied troops could go home to their families (this especially given the St. Valentine legend discussed below). But only two days before, Claudius received from Norway "entreaty, herein further shown,/That it might please you to give quiet pass/Through your dominions for this enterprise,...". He responds, "at our more considered time we'll read,/Answer, and think upon this business." 2.2.90 Given what goes on in Claudius' life in the next two days (the mousetrap, Polonius' death, Hamlet's departure), it seems unlikely that he would have had much "considered time." So Fortinbras is on the move in Denmark without Claudius' approval, which is no doubt why he sends his captain to "greet the Danish king" and crave "the conveyance of a promised march." 4.4.4 Fortinbras, like Claudius, is in a hurry.

Hamlet at Sea

With the mousetrap sequence in hand, the obvious question was how long Hamlet spent with the pirates. How much time passes between his capture and the gravedigger sequence? On digging, I discovered that the coherence of the play's chronology breaks down here. There are plenty of explicit references, as in the rest of the play, but they don't jive.

There's one explicit reference that limits how long this hiatus is. When Claudius is conscripting Laertes into his plot to kill Hamlet, he says that Lamord, a gentleman of Normandy, had spoken highly of Laertes' swordsmanship "in Hamlet's hearing…Two months since." 4.7.79, 89 This story may be a fabrication by Claudius. He's sweating at this point to win Laertes over, and flattery is his method. (And it's curious how he fishes for Laertes to provide Lamord's name.) But even if his story is false, his "two months" would have to jive with Laertes' knowledge of when Hamlet was where.

So Hamlet is gone at most two months; that's the longest possible interval between the mousetrap and gravedigger sequences, placing the gravedigger sequence in the first week of March at the latest.

Sudden and More Strange Return

But that two-month reference is contradicted in the text. Both Claudius and Hamlet refer to Hamlet's sudden return and aborted voyage, telling us that he's only been gone a couple of days—certainly less than a week. And this is in keeping with Hamlet's "Ere we were two days old at sea." Here are the key lines:

> Hamlet (in his letter to Claudius): "…my sudden and more strange return." 4.7.50

> Claudius, on reading Hamlet's letter: "What should this mean? Are all the rest come back?/…/If he be now returned,/As checking at his voyage, and that he means/No more to undertake it," 4.7.51, 66

"Checking at his voyage" sure makes it sound like Hamlet returned immediately. But the sudden return conflicts with two other items we learn in the text:

Hamlet, in his letter to Horatio: "Rosencrantz and Guildenstern hold their course for England." 4.6.12

Horatio, in the final scene of the play: "So Guildenstern and Rosencrantz go to't." 5.2.62

There are at least three problems of chronology here:

- If the ambassadors are still on their way to England when Hamlet returns, and even in the swordfight scene, how do they get back in time for the swordfight?
- How was there time for word of Polonius' death to get to Laertes in Paris, and for him to return *before* Hamlet?
- How was there time for Fortinbras to go to the "Polack wars" and return in time for the swordfight scene?

It seems impossible to reconcile those journeys with Claudius and Hamlet's language—especially since all these voyages were happening in the middle of winter, in northern Europe.

Ophelia's Flowers

There's yet another conundrum in this regard: Ophelia and her flowers. She gives a whole garden of flowers to Laertes, Claudius, and Gertrude, none of which could have been blooming in late February/early March in Denmark or in England. They could be imaginary flowers she's handing out, of course, but that doesn't solve the other Ophelia-flower problem.

In describing Ophelia's drowning, Gertrude says, "fantastic garlands did she make/Of crow-flowers, nettles, daisies, and long purples" 4.7.185. These are real summer flowers. There's no resolving that with the chronology of the play.

Gertrude does speak of a willow which "grows askant the brook/That shows his hoar leaves in the glassy stream." "Hoar" is generally interpreted as "gray," but its common usage referring to frost (cf. *A Midsummer Night's*

Dream, "The seasons alter: hoary-headed frosts/Fall in the fresh lap of the crimson rose" 2.1.111), combined with "glassy" referring to ice, could at a stretch be seen as Shakespeare giving the nod to his chronological inconsistency. Likewise, in two of her mad snatches Ophelia bumps snow right up against flowers: "White his shroud as the mountaine snow/.../Larded all with sweet flowers…" 4.5.32 and "His beard was as white as snow,/All flaxen was his pole." And Gertrude's "fantastic" could suggest that the flowers were only in Ophelia's fantasy. 4.5.160 (This literary conflation of spring and winter—with reference to Valentine's Day—was actually quite common as far back as Chaucer and before.)

Also contradictory, if interesting, is a possible source of the Ophelia drowning scene. A woman named Katherine Hamlett was drowned in the Avon near Stratford when Shakespeare was fifteen, on December 17, 1579—the dead of winter. (See below and Appendix F for more on Katherine.)

No matter whether Shakespeare was aware of these inconsistencies, or whether he acknowledged them in these passages, the contradictions are there. So for the nonce I adopted the critic's time-honored solution to contradictory evidence: I ignored it. Put aside for the moment Hamlet's "sudden and more strange return," Claudius' "checking at his voyage," and Ophelia's flowers, and we can say that Hamlet was with the pirates for as much as two months.

The Gravedigger Sequence

So with mirth in dearth and dirge in plenty (or vice versa), I'll continue. Once again, I'll resort to a table to lay out the events and references within the gravedigger sequence.

Act and Scene	Event	Text References
Day 1		
4.5	Ophelia's madness	Claudius: "Her brother is in secret come from France." 4.5.57
	Laertes bursts in.	
	Ophelia flower scene	
	Claudius convinces Laertes to listen.	

4.6	Horatio receives letters from sailors, reads his, and sends the sailors to Claudius.	Hamlet's letter to Horatio: "repair thou to me with as much speed as thou wouldest fly death." 4.6.12 Horatio to sailors: "Come, I will give you way for these your letters,/And do't the speedier that you may direct me/To him from whom you brought them." 4.6.14
4.6+ (scene in Q1 only)	Horatio's interview with Gertrude, telling her of Hamlet's return	"he hath appoynted me/To meete him on the east side of the Cittie/Tomorrow morning." Q1: 3525.8
4.7	Claudius calms (and conscripts) Laertes.	
	Messenger brings letters from Hamlet.	Hamlet's letter to Claudius: "Tomorrow shall I beg leave to see your kingly eyes." 4.7.50
	Gertrude announces Ophelia's death.	
Day 2		
5.1	Gravedigger scene	Claudius to Laertes (Q2/F1): "Strengthen your patience in our last night's speech,/We'll put the matter to the present push./.../An hour of quiet shortly shall we see;/Till then in patience our proceeding be." 5.1.186 Q1: "This very day shall Hamlet drinke his last,/For presently we meane to send to him." Q1;3496
5.2	Hamlet tells Horatio of his sea voyage.	
	Swordfight	

There are two possible hiatuses in this sequence of events:

- The time between Claudius' conversations with Laertes
- The time between the gravedigger scene and Hamlet's conversation with Horatio preceding the swordfight

The first interruption—during which Horatio receives Hamlet's letters and immediately forwards them to Claudius—must be brief, especially given all the language of haste in these scenes. Claudius is in the midst of calming a raging Laertes, who's heading a rebellious mob. He'd probably give it his immediate attention.

It's also impossible to believe that Hamlet would have long delayed telling Horatio of his packet switching on Rosencrantz and Guildenstern, or that Horatio would have waited long to hear of it. And Q1's "this very day," however dubious the source, at least demonstrates that the actor who played with Shakespeare thought that the swordfight was the same day as the graveyard scene. Combined with Q2/F1's "an hour of quiet," that reference makes it pretty likely that they're on the same day. My next discovery supports that even further.

Tomorrow Is St. Valentine's Day

After sorting out the gravedigger sequence, I kept coming back to the thorny question: When did the gravedigger sequence happen? How long was Hamlet with the pirates?

Again, a seemingly offhand reference in the text may give a clue. In her first madness scene, Ophelia sings, "To-morrow is St. Valentine's day, All in the morning betime." 4.5.39 Valentine's Day of course relates to the love/sex/ marriage themes of the play that come to a head in Ophelia's madness, but Hamlet's tossed-off "Monday morning" taught me not to gloss over such explicit statements. If this one is significant, then the graveyard and swordfight scenes the next day both occur on St. Valentine's Day—Sunday, February 14, 1602.

Elizabethans observed an ancient tradition on Valentine's Day (much deplored by the Puritans), of young people choosing partners by lot to be their valentines. As one author of the day put it, "this little Sport often ends in Love." I don't find any direct correlation to this practice in *Hamlet,* but the sexual connotations make sense, especially when you consider that images of St. Valentine often included images of cocks. The word "cock" is used six times in the play, many more if you include "woodcock," "cockle," and the like. (Yes, the *OED* cites a usage meaning "penis" as early as 1618.) One notable occurrence is Ophelia's bawdy oath—replacing "God" with "cock"—in her Valentine's song about a maid losing her virginity: "Young men will do't, if they come to't;/By Cock, they are to blame." 4.5.41

Claudius the Cruel

There are at least two unrelated St. Valentine legends. In the one that's relevant here, a Roman emperor was having trouble levying troops. He thought this was because they didn't want to leave their wives and families, so (very sensibly) he banned all marriages and engagements. Valentine, a priest, defied the ban and secretly married couples, for which he was executed. The emperor's name? Claudius II, a.k.a. "Claudius the Cruel."

The name's enough of a coincidence to raise one's eyebrows at least, and it's hard not to think of Hamlet's "I say we will have no moe marriage." 3.1.131 Just because the legend has relevance, of course, doesn't mean that the date's right. But there are several other correlations that make a lot of sense.

Two curious lines from Ophelia's madness, for instance, also lend credence:

- "How should I your true-love know/From another one?/By his cockle hat and staff,/And his sandal shoon." 4.5.27 The cockle hat refers to a cockle shell, which is essentially a souvenir worn by pilgrims who have traveled to the shrine of St. James of Compostella in Spain—a pilgrimage performed by millions over the centuries.

- "They say the owl was a baker's daughter" 4.5.37 refers to a folktale about a baker's daughter who was transformed into an owl because she begrudged Christ when he asked for some bread.

One of the saints honored on February 14 is Angelo de Gualdo (c. 1265–1325). As a youth he made the pilgrimage (barefoot!) from Italy to the shrine of St. James at Compostella. He later gave bread to the poor, which upset his mother; she subsequently died, and he felt guilty and repentant—that his action of giving bread was somehow the cause. I can find no evidence that Shakespeare knew of de Gualdo—he's a pretty obscure saint—so while it explains Ophelia's two lines, I can't recommend certainty.

Not Shriving Time Allowed

Valentine's Day was interesting in 1602, because in that year it was also Shrove Sunday, the first day of Shrovetide—the three days associated with revels, carnival, and inversion of roles ending on Shrove Tuesday. That festive tradition has its roots in the Roman Saturnalia (which, as Sohmer points out, Shakespeare was intimately familiar with through his knowledge of

Ovid's *Fasti*), and the medieval Feast of Fools with its "lords of misrule" and "boy bishops." That tradition had perhaps its highest expression in the revels—including the plays and masques—at Elizabeth's and later James' courts. The period of license (and its counterpoint, "shriving," or confession) is understandable, because the day after Shrove Tuesday is Ash Wednesday, the beginning of Lent and its forty days (plus Sundays) of abstinence leading up to Easter.

Shrovetide was the end of the revels season that starts before Christmas, and depending on which came first (Shrove Tuesday is a moveable feast calculated back from the date of Easter), either Valentine's Day or Shrovetide marked the turning point from winter to spring. In 1602 they conjoined.

Several Elizabethan Shrovetide customs are interesting regarding *Hamlet*. First—going back to the play's "cock" fixation—is the custom of "cock-throwing" or "cockthrashing." Right up there with the ever-popular bear-baiting by dogs, this game involved tying a cock to a stake, with young men throwing rocks or sticks at it. Also illuminating is the tradition of dressing up as animals, considering the series of man-and-beast passages throughout the play, some of which I cite in the Author's Preface.

But that's the tame part. At least since the 14th century, Shrovetide was intimately related to rebellion—both in fact and in "act." Crowds—especially of young men—would range through the streets in masks and costumes, raising havoc, and battles "at the ramparts" would be staged at court. By Shakespeare's day, that Shrovetide riot had taken an interesting turn. A 1630 account describes it best: "...those youths arm'd with cudgels, stones, hammers, tules, trowels, and handsawes, put the Playhouses to the sack and Bawdyhouses to the spoyle...." Various other authors mention this questionable tradition. And on Shrove Saturday, we find Laertes leading a riotous mob onto the stage of the Globe Theater.

The return of Fortinbras' army, just in time for Lent, adds a bit more weight to the dating, and the six weeks that have passed since Hamlet's departure on January 6 is a reasonable period for Laertes, the English ambassadors, and Fortinbras to have made their journeys. A further significance, perhaps spurious: Rosencrantz and Guildenstern don't make it to Shrovetide—the English king, in Hamlet's words, "those bearers put to sudden death,/Not shriving time allowed." 5.2.52

The Burial of Katherine Hamlett

Another piece of evidence, already alluded to, bears airing here—the death by drowning of (the perhaps eponymous) Katherine Hamlett near Stratford on December 17, 1579. Several authors have noted the similarity of Katherine's case to Ophelia's, especially given the gravediggers' and Laertes' commentary on the burial. There's the drowning, the question of whether it was suicide or accident, and the resulting question of whether the body could be given Christian burial. See Appendix F for a detailed discussion of these connections.

What's interesting here, once again, are the dates. Katherine Hamlett went to her final resting place sometime shortly after February 11, 1580 (when her body was "on a view" at the coroner's inquest). February 14, a Sunday, would have been propitious—especially given another unusual event: in 1580, as in 1602, February 14 was Shrove Sunday.

Julius Caesar and the Pirates

My next discovery, I think, bears narrative description to share the surpise of that discovery. This chapter, this whole book in fact, was essentially com plete. But I was nevertheless poking around in Harold Jenkins' notes and commentary to *Hamlet* (Arden, 1982) while watching my daughters' gymnastics class. In his discussion of sources Jenkins mentions Julius Caesar's being taken by pirates as a young man (recounted in Plutarch's *Lives*, which Shakespeare knew intimately both in Latin and in North's 1579 English translation). For some reason Jenkins includes Plutarch's (also oddly specific) statement that Caesar was with the pirates for thirty-eight days.

I laid Jenkins' book in my lap and looked up, calculating the time passage from January 7, when Hamlet is taken by the pirates, to February 13, when he returns. And I sat in stunned silence, realizing that the duration, calculated inclusively as was the Roman practice, is in fact thirty-eight days.

This simply cannot be coincidence. I didn't start with thirty-eight days and go looking for dates that fit. The whole calendar conceit of this chapter was complete before I ever came upon Jenkins' mention. The surety of Plutarch as a source is even firmer when you look at how well both Caesar and Hamlet get on with the pirates. I discuss this in more detail, and quote the passage from Plutarch, in Chapter Five.

I had written a fairly qualified conclusion to this section on the "pirate gap," suggesting that February 14 is well supported as a date for the graveyard, but not so well supported as other aspects of the chronology. After discovering the duration of Caesar's pirate sojourn in Plutarch, though, I find the evidence to be irrefutable. The graveyard scene is on February 14.

Shrovetide Revels at Court

Like Twelfth Night, Shrovetide was one of the key holidays when plays were performed at court, and at other institutions like the inns of court and the universities. In the forty-two years 1567–1608, there were plays at court at Shrovetide every year but four—often multiple performances. Two of those four missing years include possible performances, and the other two—1593 and 1594—were notorious plague years when the playing companies were in disarray. In the twelve years 1596–1607, eight of the Shrovetide perform-ances were by Shakespeare's company.

One other year was especially notable. On February 14, 1613—yet an-other year in which Valentine's Day fell on Shrove Sunday—Princess Eliza-beth, daughter of James I and Anne of Denmark and patron of Lady Eliza-beth's Men, was married to Frederick V (who at the time took over patron-age of Prince Henry's Men, Henry having just died). The event was sur-rounded by weeks of revels, including a full twenty performances by Shake-speare's company.

Finally, it is at least interesting to note that on Shrove Sunday, February 14, 1602, Shakespeare's company played before the court at Whitehall. We don't know what play they presented. It's nice to think it was *Hamlet*.

The Christmas Prince

One more table, summarizing the events from the murder to the swordfight, should help lay out the whole chronology of the play (again, see the graphi-cal timeline). You can take the actual dates for what you will (though the ghost's reappearance on Twelfth Night and Caesar's thirty-eight days with the pirates are, for me at least, quite convincing). The durations—aside from how long Hamlet was with the pirates—are unambiguously stated in the text.

1601		
Sunday, September 6	Old Hamlet murdered	
Tuesday, September 8		John Shakespeare buried

Sunday, October 4	Claudius and Gertrude married	
Friday, October 30	The ghost walks.	Feast of Marcellus
Saturday, October 31	The ghost walks.	All Hallows Eve
Sunday, November 1	The ghost walks.	All Saints' Day
Monday, November 2	Court scene Laertes, Voltemand, and Cornelius depart. The ghost walks.	All Souls' Day
1602		
Monday, January 4	Ambassadors return. The players arrive.	
Tuesday, January 5	Mousetrap The ghost walks.	Twelfth Night
Wednesday, January 6	Hamlet and English ambassadors depart. Fortinbras departs for Poland.	Epiphany
Thursday, January 7	Hamlet taken by pirates.	
Saturday, February 13	Ophelia's madness. Laertes returns. Hamlet's letters arrive.	
Sunday, February 14	Hamlet returns. Graveyard and swordfight Fortinbras returns. English ambassadors return.	Valentine's Day Shrove Sunday

The action of *Hamlet* begins October 31, Halloween, has its middle on January 5, Twelfth Night, and ends on February 14, Shrove Sunday/Valentine's Day. It's tempting and amusing to find in this Shakespeare's complex response to Ben Jonson and other learned types, who insisted on a rather simplistic version of Aristotle's "unity of time"—that a play's action should span no more than a single day—and that it should have a beginning, a middle, and an end.

It's also interesting to see this span in relation to the season of revels discussed in this chapter. We have two especially detailed documents describing revels seasons, and the reigns of "Christmas princes" or "lords of mis-

rule"—mock sovereigns, with all the powers, pomp, prerogatives, and ap-
purtenances of office.

The first account, reported in *Gesta Grayorum*, is of the reign of Henry
Helmes, the "Prince of Purpoole," at Gray's Inn (one of the Inns of Court—
residential law schools/societies of London) in 1594/95. The revels began
December 20, and on December 28 ("Innocents Day at night") *Comedy of
Errors* was played by Shakespeare's company. The revels continued until
Twelfth Night, then they resumed on Candlemas (February 2), and a con-
cluded with a mask presented before the Queen at Whitehall at Shrovetide
(Monday or Tuesday). There was also that night a simulated battle defending
the ramparts against "rebels," the Prince of Purpoole taking sides with the
Earl of Cumberland against the Earl of Essex and others. The next day, the
maskers were presented to the queen, and the Prince's reign ended.

The other account is of the 1607/8 season at St. John's College, Oxford
(not to be confused with St. John's College, Cambridge, which I discuss in
some detail in Chapter Four and Appendix B). In this account a certain
Thomas Tucker was invested "Christmas Lord or Prince of the Revels" on
All Hallows Eve at night, All Saint's Eve, Saturday, October 31, 1607. His
reign ended, and he resigned his crown, on Shrove Tuesday, February 9,
1608. A final play was then performed on Saturday, February 13, the eve of
St. Valentine's Day. His reign aligns exactly with the period of Claudius'
"misrule" and its drunken revelry, exactly six years later—and with Hamlet's
reign as the Christmas Prince.

Hamlet and Hamnet

All this dating leads to yet another connection with Shakespeare's life. Will's
only son, Hamnet, was christened along with his twin sister Judith on February 2, 1585 (Candlemas). Hamnet died at age 11; he was buried August 11,
1596.

"Hamnet" and "Hamlet" were basically interchangeable in the spelling-
challenged Elizabethan age (Shaxpere's name was spelled every which way
from Sunday). For example: Hamnet Sadler was Shakespeare's Stratford
neighbor, lifelong friend, and a legatee in his will. (He got twenty-six shil-
lings and eight pence for the purchase of a ring—a traditional bequest also
given to Will's colleagues Heminges, Burbage, and Condell.) Sadler's wife
was Judith, so they presumably served as namesakes and godparents for the
twins. And in Shakespeare's will (the second draft, at that), Hamnet Sadler is

referred to as both "Hamlett" and "Hamnet." The switch was run-of-the-mill.

If we equate young Hamnet Shakespeare's birthday with young Hamlet's, then Hamlet is sixteen at the beginning of the play, and he dies just after his seventeenth birthday.

And when 37-year-old Will Shakespeare sat down in the Fall of 1601 to revise this most mortality-laden of all plays, so larded with fathers and sons, his father had just died, and that just a month after the fifth anniversary of Hamnet's death—his only son.

Puzzling the Will

So why does all this chronology matter? Of what importance are all these relationships, connections, and connotations, aside from the clever feeling you get from solving a crossword puzzle?

The answer, for me, lies in the added complexity, coherence, and resulting richness that's revealed in the play when you understand the web of time and date references. That understanding adds layers of interwoven meanings that are immanent in the all-pervasive Elizabethan liturgical calendar, and illuminates the very personal events that informed the creation of the play.

At the very least, this analysis explains the basic action of the play—who does what and when—an explanation that's fundamental to understanding its deeper import. And that's the subject of the remaining chapters: the import of Hamlet's youth, the youth of those around him, and the plethora of date and time references that "riddle" the play.

CHAPTER THREE

A Certain Convocation of Politic Worms

In Chapter One I laid out all sorts of "hard" evidence showing that Hamlet must be a teen. But the real evidence is the play itself, the characters in the play, the action of the play, and how they all interact. If Hamlet's a teen, all sorts of things about the play—from overarching themes to troublesome jokes that seem to be missing their punch lines—make sense in a way that they just plain don't if he's thirty. A lot of that "sense" has to do with Hamlet's political situation.

A good question to begin with is one that critics and fans have been asking forever: why didn't Hamlet succeed to the throne immediately on his father's death? Why, how, and when did Claudius take the throne? There has been much throwing about of brains on the subject—elective versus successive monarchy in Denmark and Elizabethan England, power versus privilege, Hamlet's illegitimacy, etc., etc. To add my farthing's part, if Hamlet hasn't achieved majority, it reduces his power base, adds the complications of a regent or protector (Claudius? Polonius?), and in general helps explain why he didn't have the oomph to take the throne on his father's death.

Go Not to Mine Uncle's Bed

But whatever the reason, succession is a crux of the play. And if it's a crux, so is Hamlet's age, because if Hamlet is a teen, then Gertrude is in her early thirties. She could bear Claudius a rival heir. (Shakespeare's mother Mary bore her first child circa age eighteen, and her last at about forty.) This assumes she married as a teen (at Ophelia's age), which is what you'd expect for royalty in those times.

Arguably contradicting this are Hamlet's words to Gertrude in the closet scene: "...at your age/The heyday in the blood is tame, it's humble,/And waits upon the judgment." 3.4.78 But those words make most sense in the Elizabethan age—when the average life expectancy (at birth) was only 40—if they're contrasting a teenager to a 33-year-old. (The average marriage age for common folk in Shakespeare's day was in the mid twenties, but for dynastic and political reasons, the aristocracy, and especially royalty, married quite young.)

No critic that I've read has realized this implication of Gertrude's youth. The only way Claudius could cement his power, throne, and dynasty would be to produce a male heir. Gertrude's ability to bear a child ratchets the intensity of the succession struggle up several notches.

The courtiers of Elsinore would be intensely sensitive to that political reality, as would London theatergoers, schooled as they were by endless reenactments of the Wars of the Roses, which were about succession and nothing but succession. (Not to mention the ongoing and decidedly fatal dynastic machinations of Elizabeth and her serially matrimonial father, who was so obsessed with producing a male heir.) I tallied it up: of the twenty-two plays that Shakespeare wrote before *Hamlet*, twelve were all about wars of succession, and succession plays an important part in a large handful of others.

The importance of succession in the play rings even more true when you consider the lengths to which Shakespeare himself went in his will to ensure that his full estate would pass to a single male descendant, even though his only male heir—his son Hamnet—had died in 1596, twenty years before Will's death. I just have to share a brief snippet from the endless masculine declensions in Will's will:

"...unto the said Susanna Hall [Will's married daughter]...& after her decease to the first son of her bodie...& so to the heirs Males of

the body of the said second sone...and for default of such issue...to
the fourth fifth sixth and seventh sons...and to the heirs males...of
the bodies of the said fourth fifth sixth & seventh sons..."

When I realized how important Gertrude's ability to bear a male heir is
to the motivations in the play, I started looking more closely at the political
situation in Denmark. And it quickly became clear that Claudius is in a
shaky situation politically, right from the beginning of the play—no matter
how masterfully he glosses it over. And young Hamlet is at the heart of his
problems. As Queen Elizabeth knew all too well (from both sides of the issue), a successor with a valid claim to the throne is always a magnet for rival
factions. And young Hamlet is far more attractive metal than most.

While Hamlet's threat to Claudius' life and throne isn't stated explicitly
until later in the play—even by Hamlet—that threat is present and palpable
from the beginning. That ever-present undercurrent explains many words
and actions in the play that otherwise seem inexplicable or troublesome.

Something Is Rotten in the State of Denmark

Let's start by looking at what the play tells us about Hamlet's Denmark.
First, it's not just a state, it's a small empire. A good chunk of Norway's ter-
ritory is under Danish control, surrendered upon old Fortinbras' defeat by
old Hamlet in single combat. (Horatio explains this in the opening scene.
1.1.96) England is a tribute state, at the beck of the Danish king (cf. Claudius'
references to England: "demand of our neglected tribute" 3.1.152, and "thy
free awe/Pays homage to us" 4.3.55) And presumably a slice of Poland is under Denmark's sway as well, from when old Hamlet "smote the sledded
Polacks on the ice." 1.1.79

But the empire is under attack—seemingly just since King Hamlet's
death. Horatio tells us that Fortinbras has "Shark'd up a list of lawless resolutes,/...to some enterprise/...which is no other,/As it doth well appear unto
our state,/But to recover of us" the lands that Fortinbras' father lost to old
Hamlet. 1.1.118 What's odd here is that Bernardo and Marcellus—officers,
not just soldiers—have to ask what the sudden and hurried arming of the
state is all about 1.1.86:

Good now, sit down, and tell me, he that knows,
Why this same strict and most observant watch

So nightly toils the subject of the land,
And why such daily cast of brazen cannon,
And foreign mart for implements of war,
Why such impress of shipwrights, whose sore task
Does not divide the Sunday from the week,
What might be toward, that this sweaty haste
Doth make the night joint-laborer with the day:
Who is't that can inform me?

They're at a loss for what's going on, and their command structure is so uncertain that they don't know who to ask. This uneasy uncertainty is emphasized by the repetitive "tell me he that knows" and "Who is't that can inform me" in the first and last lines of the passage.

This repetition epitomizes the anxious uncertainty that echoes through Elsinore—from the opening "Who's there?"—which I discuss at some length in Chapter Five. The repetition is also a technique to keep the audience's attention during this discursive explanation (like Prospero's constant "are you listening?" interjections in his explanatory first scene with Miranda in *The Tempest*). But if you trust the coherence of Shakespeare's narrative and his ability to use dialogue for multiple purposes, that's beside the point; it puts across the unsettled political situation in Denmark. Claudius echoes this muddied state—or the international perception of it—in the opening court scene: "...young Fortinbras,/Holding a weak supposal of our worth,/ Or thinking by our late dear brother's death/Our state to be disjoint and out of frame...." 1.2.19

England, likewise, is not a stable Danish client. Claudius' "Since yet thy cicatrice [scar] looks raw and red/After the Danish sword" 4.3.55 tells us that it was only recently conquered or brought back into line, and his reference to "demand of our neglected tribute" (four months after King Hamlet's death) 3.1.152 shows that Denmark's dominion over England is far from sound.

Hamlet the Heir

So Claudius has external problems on his hands. But from the first lines of the play, the real threat is Hamlet. In Belleforest's and Saxo Grammaticus' versions, the prince's reason for feigning madness is explicitly to diminish himself as a challenger to the throne, and avoid being offed by the king before he can "attain to man's estate" and take his revenge and his rightful crown. And our Hamlet has strong support in the army and the citizenry.

The Guards' Allegiance. When Marcellus and Bernardo encounter the ghost, as Horatio says, "This to me/In dreadful secrecy impart they did." 1.2.206 They don't tell their superiors, or King Claudius; they intentionally keep it secret from them. They tell Horatio—young Prince Hamlet's college buddy, a person with no real position at court. (Hamlet: "For what advancement may I hope from thee/That no revenue hast but thy good spirits/To feed and clothe thee?" 3.2.21) It's no wonder their subordinate Francisco is "sick at heart," 1.1.11 when his officers are unclear about where their allegiances should lie.

After seeing the ghost, Horatio asks Marcellus and Bernardo of Hamlet, "Do you consent we shall acquaint him with it,/As needful in our loves, fit ting our duty?" 1.1.192 Then when they tell Hamlet, Horatio says, "...we did think it writ down in our duty /To let you know of it." 1.2.234 The officers join with Horatio in duty to Hamlet, not to Claudius.

Hamlet's comradeship with the officers is augmented later by his "I have been in continual practice" at fencing. 5.2.143 For who should he have been practicing with—we know it's not Horatio, Laertes, Rosencrantz, or Guildenstern—except officers of the guard? It's also shown by Marcellus' seeking call to Hamlet after the ghost encounter—"Illo, ho, ho, my Lord!", and by Hamlet's reply: "Hillo, ho, ho, boy! Come, bird, come." 1.5.125 Both are cries of a falconer to summon his hawk; they apparently hunt together.

It's also notable that when Laertes storms in heading a mob, Claudius calls on his "Swissers" 4.5.68 to protect him—hired Swiss mercenaries, not officers of the Danish guard. Again, it's no wonder that Claudius is worried about Hamlet, if the army is allegiant to the young prince.

The People's Allegiance. Claudius tells Laertes explicitly that he couldn't respond to Hamlet's killing of Polonius as he would have liked, or present the true facts to the people ("Why to a public count I might not go") because of "the great love the general gender bear him." 4.7.21 He continues, "...my arrows,/Too slightly timber'd for so loud a wind,/Would have reverted to my bow again." As Hamlet says of Claudius, there were "those that would make mouths at him while my father liv'd." 2.2.268 He's not well timbered, politically; the people are ready to supplant him, as shown in the courtier's announcement of Laertes' arrival back from France: 4.5.70

> Save yourself, my lord!
> ...young Laertes, in a riotous head,
> O'erbears your officers. The rabble call him lord,
> ...
> They cry, "Choose we, Laertes shall be king!"
> Caps, hands, and tongues applaud it to the clouds,
> "Laertes shall be king, Laertes king!"

In Claudius' words, the people are "muddied/Thick and unwholesome in their thoughts and whispers." 4.5.50 And Horatio, the voice of peace, plain dealing, and moderation, repeatedly tells us likewise. When he's asked if he can tell why the country is arming, he replies, "That can I,/At least the whisper goes so," 1.1.97 and proceeds to describe the "post-haste and romage [turmoil] in the land." 1.1.124 Later, he speaks of the evil omens that preceded Caesar's death: "...even the like precurse of fear'd events,/.../Have heaven and earth together demonstrated/Unto our climatures and countrymen." 1.1.138 In convincing Gertrude to speak to the mad Ophelia, he says, "'Twere good she were spoken with, for she may strew/Dangerous conjectures in ill-breeding minds." 4.5.17

The air of whispers, scuttlebutt, and wicked rumor is also apparent in Laertes' confusion about how his father died. In Claudius' words, Laertes: 4.5.59

> . . . wants not buzzers to infect his ear
> With pestilent speeches of his father's death,
> Wherein necessity, of matter beggar'd,
> Will nothing stick our person to arraign
> In ear and ear.

Lacking facts, the rumors indict Claudius, not Hamlet. In Q1's corrupt if revealing text, Claudius says of Laertes at this point, "he hath halfe the heart of all our Land." Q1: 2825.1 Laertes, no longer having a father to rein him in as the elder Norway curbs his nephew Fortinbras, takes advantage of this, and like Fortinbras, sharks up a list of lawless resolutes to some enterprise that hath a stomach in it. The people are ready to follow a fiery leader—be it Laertes, Hamlet, or presumably even Fortinbras.

Laertes' brief rebellion is less than four months after the opening court scene, and it makes clear that even in that earlier scene, Claudius' claim to the people's allegiance was far from strong—especially compared to Hamlet's.

Chiefest Courtier, Cousin, and Our Son

In this light, it's worth taking another look at the court scene in Act 1 1.2. It appears to be the king's first open court since the "o'erhasty marriage" and coronation, and he runs through several pieces of official business. Chief among these is his proclamation of Hamlet's political position: "Let the world take note/You are the most immediate to our throne." 1.2.112

But given that Claudius has, in Hamlet's words, "popp'd in between th'election and my hopes," 5.2.72 and given Gertrude's potential to bear a rival heir, Claudius' seemingly generous proclamation of Hamlet's political position rings more than a bit hollow. Hamlet's very first line in the play is a multiply ironic comment on that dynastic situation, responding to Claudius's "my cousin Hamlet, and my son": "A little more than kin, and less than kind." 1.2.67-68

Return to Wittenberg

There are two other pieces of business that Claudius attends to in the opening court scene that are of moment here: Laertes' and Hamlet's requests to return to school (one of many such dualities in the play). Claudius accedes to Laertes' request, but denies Hamlet's—albeit with candied tongue and the help of Gertrude's entreaties.

It's a time-honored practice to keep your challengers close, where you can keep an eye on them, so it's no wonder that Claudius finds Hamlet's request "most retrograde to our desire." 1.2.118 (The irony is that it's Laertes, not Hamlet, who returns in secret, heading a rebellion.) Claudius only decides that Hamlet should leave after the nunnery scene, in which Claudius detects "...something in his soul/.../Will be some danger; which for to prevent,/.../...he shall with speed to England." 3.1.147 Hamlet the successor eventually becomes more dangerous in his presence than in his missioned absence.

The Pate of a Politician

So Hamlet makes Claudius nervous, and so he should. He is, in Ophelia's words, "Th'expectancy and rose of the fair state." 3.1.134 He certainly has a stronger claim to the throne than Fortinbras or Laertes—who actively attempt to seize it—and he's far more popular with the army and the populace than Claudius is.

But young Hamlet begins the play as a remarkably unpolitical beast, which is one of the reasons we like him so much. He's much more concerned with the personal and familial; he's his mother's son in this regard. Three examples:

- Hamlet's first soliloquy—"O that this too too sullied/sallied/solid flesh" 1.2.133—is all about Gertrude's posting "with such dexterity to incestious sheets." 1.2.161 He doesn't even mention the succession or the throne.

- In his ensuing conversation with Horatio, Marcellus, and Bernardo, he cracks wise that "the funeral bak'd-meats/Did coldly furnish forth the marriage tables," 1.2.186 but makes no allusion to having been supplanted.

- Even Claudius, assuring Laertes while plotting Hamlet's death late in the play, describes Hamlet as "remiss,/Most generous, and free from all contriving." 4.7.148

Immediately on being told of the ghost's appearance, though, Hamlet senses the danger of his situation, and he starts to get wise politically. He immediately enjoins Bernardo, Marcellus, and Horatio to secrecy: 1.2.266

If you have hitherto conceal'd this sight,
Let it be tenable in your silence still;
And whatsomever else shall hap to-night,
Give it an understanding, but no tongue:

Then after the ghost's revelation, he repeatedly (repeatedly!) swears Marcellus and Horatio to secrecy. The ghost, knowing Hamlet's danger better than any other, offers no little help with his repeated "Swear!" And it's here that Hamlet conceives his notion to feign madness.

From this point on, Hamlet chafes constantly at having been displaced. He already knew he couldn't comment on the hasty marriage ("But break my heart, for I must hold my tongue" 1.2.163). But starting with the ghost's revelation, he begins his gibes on that most dangerous of subjects—the succession. And he quickly reveals that he's not a complete ingenue; all those gibes are cloaked in a self-protective cloud of quibble and obfuscation.

In Hamlet's first scene following the ramparts, the succession topic arises almost immediately, when Rosencrantz and Guildenstern arrive. The three start with their college-boys' banter about the strumpet Fortune sending them to Denmark. Then when Hamlet says, "Denmark's a prison," 2.2.228 they faux-innocently argue with him ("Then is the world one," and "We think not so, my lord"), as if they weren't completely wise to Hamlet's galling political position.

Within a few lines, they turn discussion to Hamlet's "ambition," and Hamlet barely skirts the succession issue in reply: "I could be bounded in a nutshell, and count myself a king of infinite space." 2.2.234 Rosencrantz goes on about ambition, despising it as "but a shadow's shadow." These heavy-handed sallies tip Hamlet to their allegiances. When they admit that they were sent for, he feeds them disinformation to take back to Claudius, turning their own, and Claudius', style of faux innocence back upon them: "I have of late—but wherefore I know not—lost all my mirth, forgone all custom of exercises...." 2.2.250

The Very Cunning of the Scene

It was a long time before I realized that Hamlet's disinformation campaign continues in the next scene as well, and I came understand what's really going on in the 800-pound gorilla of all soliloquies: "To be or not to be." Almost everybody—critics, directors, and others, myself included—has been blind to the cunning that is at play in that scene, and that speech. Then I came across a paper by James Hirsh presented at a Globe Theatre conference on *Hamlet* in 2001 (plus two of his previous papers cited therein). Hirsh points out the stunningly obvious: When Hamlet delivers that soliloquy, Claudius and Polonius are in the room, concealed. And Hamlet knows it (or certainly suspects it). He's playing to the king.

Few have cared to consider that the most lauded passage in English literature is not, in fact, the eloquent and truthful outpouring of a noble heart, but a brilliant act of dissimulation and deceit. Unlike Hamlet's recital of the Hecuba speech in the previous scene, at this point he is "acting" in deadly earnest.

Directors have gone through incredible contortions to avoid such staging. But the evidence of the text—clouded at least since the Restoration by the speech's adoption as a leading man's oratorical set-piece—makes it clear that something much more complex is at play than Hamlet unpacking his profound inner thoughts and feelings.

I'll only mention a couple of Hirsh's key points, showing that Hamlet knows of Claudius' (and/or Polonius') presence, that what we see as an audience is "an elaborate eavesdropping episode"—very common in Shakespearean and all Elizabethan drama—and showing how the soliloquy serves Hamlet's turn.

The central point is that Hamlet arrives because Claudius has sent for him: "For we have closely sent for Hamlet hither,/That he, as 'twere by accident, may here/Affront Ophelia." 3.1.36 Hamlet has just finished unmasking his schoolfellows and plotting the mousetrap; his suspicions are at a peak. So while he may not know that Claudius, Polonius, or both are in the room (the play's opening line, "Who's there?" 1.1.3 reverberates here as well), he sure knows it's probable. The scene can be staged so he actually sees them hide, without departing the text(s).

An additional point that Hirsh doesn't mention: Unlike F1, in Q2 there is no "exeunt" stage direction for Claudius and Polonius before Hamlet's entrance; they could actually be "concealed" on stage. (Ophelia is overtly present in both versions.) There is no such stage direction for Gertrude either, however (in either version), though she clearly exits at Claudius' behest. Stage directions are spotty in all the editions, so take this for what it's worth.

In the soliloquy, Hamlet doesn't mention the succession, the marriage, the murder, or the ghost. (On the latter, he in fact speaks of "The undiscover'd country from whose bourn/No traveller returns.") Rather he delivers what is truly the stylized set-speech of an Elizabethan melancholic—formal, philosophic, and "utterly impersonal." He doesn't once use a first-person singular, as he does constantly in every other soliloquy. As Hirsh says, "Hamlet pretends to give them precisely what they have been seeking, a reliable account of what is troubling him." He "attempts to lull Claudius into a false sense of security by declaring himself incapable of taking action." And (my addition), he suggests that he might just solve Claudius' problem for him, "with a bare bodkin."

Hamlet's dissimulation isn't entirely effective, though—mainly because he loses his cool with Ophelia. He tips his hand to the eavesdroppers, and scuttles his own deception, with his "Where's your father?" 3.1.125 and "those that are married already, all but one, shall live" 3.1.131 Claudius is no fool; he comments after the nunnery scene: 3.1.145

> Love! his affections do not that way tend;
> Nor what he spake, though it lack'd form a little,
> Was not like madness. There's something in his soul
> O'er which his melancholy sits on brood;
> And, I do doubt, the hatch and the disclose
> Will be some danger;

Playing to Polonius, who doesn't know of the murder, Claudius pretends to take Hamlet's soliloquy and madness at face value, to justify sending him to England: 3.1.151

> I have in quick determination
> Thus set it down: he shall with speed to England,
> For the demand of our neglected tribute:
> Haply the seas and countries different
> With variable objects shall expel
> This something-settled matter in his heart,
> Whereon his brains still beating puts him thus
> From fashion of himself.

The flaw is apparent here, and Claudius' intentions are clear, probably even to Polonius. Would Claudius send a mad youth, the greatest threat to his crown, to deal with a recalcitrant subject king? (This isn't Philip sending 18-year-old Alexander to state terms to the defeated Athenians.) In fact, Claudius senses what we should also sense—that he's *not* hearing Hamlet's inmost thoughts: "There's something in his soul"—beneath his stylized melancholy. What Claudius really fears is what is in fact the case: that Hamlet knows something he's not revealing, and that "the hatch and the disclose/Will be some danger." In the mousetrap, Claudius discovers that fear to be all too well founded.

Hirsh's insight into the "To be" soliloquy is sad news for those aging, sonorous leading men that insist on taking the part of this young prince, and for those who would cling to the romantically idealized Hamlet (and Shake-

speare). But for those actors, directors, playgoers, and readers who care
more for drama than declamation, Hirsh's reading reveals an exquisite tension in the scene, a tension that has been felt only rarely, if at all, since the
days of Shakespeare's Globe.

A final note: I have to wonder if Shakespeare realized just how funny we
would find it, after listening to this oh-so-formal of soliloquies, a passage
that has attained to the loftiest of literary aeries, to hear Claudius say, Polo-
nius-like, that "it lack'd form a little."

No few commentators of Shakespeare's day and after (from Jonson to
Johnson, and beyond) have said the same about Shakespeare's work in general.

Chameleon's Dish

The barely hidden power play between Hamlet and Claudius continues in
the next scene—ostensibly their first time together since the opening court
scene—when Claudius enters for the mousetrap. And the tension from their
previous "encounter" builds even further. Hamlet immediately plays on
Claudius' "fares," and jabs at his own displacement, with his very first line:
3.2.58

> King: How fares our cousin Hamlet?
>
> Hamlet: Excellent, i'faith, of the chameleon's dish: I eat the air,
> promise-cramm'd;—you cannot feed capons so.

As all the annotated editions tell us, chameleons were thought to live on
air, and Hamlet, likewise, is living on "heir"—surviving on nothing but
Claudius' crammed promise that "you are the most immediate to our
throne." 1.2.112 The "capons" line, on the other hand, goes unexplained in
almost every edition. It's unfortunate, because I find in it a *treble entendre* (at
least): it plays on the provender needed to fatten a bird (as Jenkins notes,
Hamlet is crammed with promises only), but also on capons being gelded:
young Hamlet is both starved and unmanned by his position. And it hints of
Hamlet being fattened for the slaughter. ("We fat all creatures else to fat us,
and we fat ourselves for maggots." 4.3.26) Finally, "capon" speaks of a dull
fool. (See for instance *Comedy of Errors:* "capon, coxcomb, idiot, patch!"
3.1.32) Hamlet is saying, "you can't treat fools thus; do you think you can

handle me so?" It's even denser when you see all this passing between two who are squaring off like fighting cocks in the pits of the Southwark theater district.

Just after the mousetrap, Hamlet again engages Rosencrantz and Guildenstern on the succession issue, with his "I lack advancement." 3.2.250 Rosencrantz protests, "How can that be, when you have the voice of the King himself for your succession in Denmark?" Hamlet disdains that voice: "Ay, sir, but 'While the grass grows.'" The traditional proverb continues, "…the steed starves." Hamlet again casts himself bitterly as a domesticated animal. And again, food is the metaphor—succession as sustenance.

Then in the closet with Gertrude he's at it again, calling Claudius "A cutpurse of the empire and the rule,/That from a shelf the precious diadem stole/And put it in his pocket." 3.4.113 And to Horatio in the final scene, he says, "He that hath kill'd my king and whor'd my mother,/Popp'd in between th' election and my hopes,/Thrown out his angle [as in angler] for my proper life." 5.2.71 The succession isn't the only thing bothering Hamlet, but it's certainly one thing.

Denmark's a Prison

Given his political situation, Hamlet's "Denmark's a prison" 2.2.228 might be more literal than figurative. To begin with, of course, Claudius won't allow him to return to Wittenberg. The threat of imprisonment is explicit in Polonius' line to Claudius ("If she [Gertrude] find him not,/To England send him, or confine him where/Your wisdom best shall think." 3.1.168), and in Rosencrantz's line to Hamlet ("You do surely bar the door upon your own liberty if you deny your griefs to your friend." 3.2.249). That sense of imprisonment arises again in Hamlet's report of his enforced night at sea: "Methought I lay/Worse than the mutines in the bilboes. [mutineers in fetters]" 5.2.7

So from the time of the Ghost's revelation, and throughout the play, Hamlet chafes at Claudius' usurping the throne, and his own resulting "bilboes." But even more, on a personal level he resents both the politics of the Danish court and the political faction that supports Claudius—a faction that's centered on Polonius and his clan.

Counselor Most Secret and Most Grave

Our first hint as to Polonius' allegiances comes in the opening court scene, when Claudius speaks of the hasty marriage: "...nor have we herein barr'd/ Your better wisdoms, which have freely gone/With this affair along." 1.2.16 A bow to Polonius is probably in order when this line's delivered. Claudius is spinning the situation to his best advantage; not everyone in Denmark has gone along so freely as Polonius.

Polonius really comes clear, though, in his interchange with Gertrude and Claudius about Hamlet and Ophelia: 2.2.136

Claudius: But how hath she/Receiv'd his love?

Polonius: What do you think of me?

Claudius: As of a man faithful and honorable.

Polonius then asks, with notable prolixity that I've elided here, "...what might you,/...think,/If I.../...look'd upon this love with idle sight,/...?"

The answer, of course, is that if Polonius encouraged or allowed a match between Hamlet and Ophelia—which could result in a rival heir—Claudius would think him aligned with Hamlet, not "faithful and honorable." Showing his good faith, Polonius reports that he "went round to work" and forbade Ophelia from accepting Hamlet's letters or advances. Polonius' "take this from this [his head from his body] if this be otherwise" emphasizes his faithfulness to the death (as it turns out...). Right up to his death, Polonius is Claudius' main supporter and co-conspirator. And even after his death, his son Laertes takes over the role. (At the beginning of the play, Laertes tells Claudius that he returned from Paris not for Hamlet's funeral, or for Gertrude's wedding, but "I came to Denmark/To show my duty in your coronation." 1.2.52)

Polonius is right that "...this brain of mine/Hunts not the trail of policy so sure/As it hath us'd to do" 2.2.52—especially up against Claudius' consumate manipulation and Hamlet's brilliance—but Polonius is a political animal through and through. This goes a long way toward explaining Hamlet's behavior toward him. Before I could really understand that behavior, though, I had to look at Hamlet's relationship to Ophelia.

Sweet Nymph

Hamlet's "I did love you once" 3.1.121 in the nunnery scene, and Ophelia's "Indeed, my lord, you made me believe so" in reply, plus other matter in the play, tells us that they were lovers once, if not physically then at least emotionally. "'Tis told me," says Polonius—forever with an ear to the ground—that Hamlet "hath very oft of late/Given private time to you, and you yourself/Have of your audience been most free and bounteous." 1.3.99

Laertes and Polonius bring that relationship to a sudden end just after the opening court scene. Their reasons are revealingly similar, if ultimately twisted and specious.

Laertes tells Ophelia to view Hamlet's love as "...not permanent, sweet, not lasting," 1.3.11 because "...his will is not his own,/For he himself is subject to his birth:/He may not, as unvalued persons do,/Carve for himself, for on his choice depends/The safety and health of this whole state." 1.3.22 Hamlet's promises can be believed "...no further/Than the main voice of Denmark goes withal." 1.3.33 And where goes the main voice of Denmark (read: Claudius), there goes Laertes, and his father. Hamlet later toys with Polonius for this—Polonius' opinions shifting with the political winds, the whims of royalty: 3.2.268

> Hamlet: Do you see yonder cloud that's almost in shape of a camel?
>
> Polonius: By th' mass and 'tis, like a camel indeed.
>
> Hamlet: Methinks it is like a weasel.
>
> Polonius: It is back'd like a weasel.
>
> Hamlet: Or like a whale.
>
> Polonius: Very like a whale.

Hamlet does the same thing to Osric later in the play: 5.2.96

> Osric: I thank your lordship, 'tis very hot.

Hamlet: No, believe me, 'tis very cold; the wind is northerly.

Osric: It is indifferent cold, my lord, indeed.

Hamlet: But yet methinks it is very sultry and hot for my complexion.

Osric: Exceedingly, my lord; it is very sultry, as 'twere, I cannot tell how.

Polonius is a sycophant to royalty (like Osric), but he's also a more sophisticated persuader than Laertes. He warns Ophelia that Hamlet is just trying to seduce her; his vows are "mere implorators of unholy suits." 1.3.137 But when he later reports this conversation to Claudius, the admonition he claims to have given is "'Lord Hamlet is a prince out of thy star;/This must not be.'" 2.2.150

Both father and brother say that Hamlet is an unacceptable suitor for Ophelia. But a line from Gertrude in the graveyard puts the lie to their calumny: "I hop'd thou shouldst have been my Hamlet's wife./I thought thy bride-bed to have deck'd, sweet maid,/And not have strew'd thy grave." 5.1.126 Hamlet obviously felt likewise; Ophelia tells Polonius that Hamlet "hath importun'd me with love/In honourable fashion...hath given countenance to his speech, my lord,/With almost all the holy vows of heaven." 1.3.110

Before King Hamlet's murder and Claudius' accession, Hamlet and Ophelia were considered a fine match. Their dalliances were at least tolerated, if not encouraged. But Laertes and Polonius warn Ophelia off because such a match would put their family in Hamlet's camp—directly at odds with Claudius.

So it's no wonder that Hamlet is furious. He's a teenager in love, jilted and cut off without a word of explanation, his missives refused, for political reasons that are painfully obvious to him. When he gets really abusive—repeatedly telling Ophelia to get to a nunnery, which was slang for a whorehouse—we might not like it, but we can certainly understand it in a teen smitten by the pangs of despised love. We can understand it even more when we consider that Polonius and Claudius are at that moment lurking and listening, and that Hamlet knows it—that his ex-lover is conniving with his lethal enemy against him.

Hamlet's first meeting with Polonius—shortly before the nunnery scene—also comes clear in this light. 2.2.189

> Polonius: Do you know me, my lord?
>
> Hamlet: Excellent well, you are a fishmonger.
>
> Polonius: Not I, my lord.
>
> Hamlet: Then I would you were so honest a man.

"Fishmonger" is Elizabethan cant for "fleshmonger"—a pimp, procurer, or bawd. In Hamlet's view, Polonius treats Ophelia as so much flesh for barter—and rightly so, given Polonius' "I'll loose my daughter to him," 2.2.175 as if she's a mare for the breeding. But Polonius is even less honest than a bawd; he manipulates Ophelia for political capital, not just time-honored pecuniary reasons.

Later, in the scene when the players arrive, Hamlet confounds Polonius with his ramblings on Jephthah: 2.2.285

> Hamlet: O Jephthah, judge of Israel, what a treasure hadst thou!
>
> Polonius: What a treasure had he, my lord?
>
> Hamlet: Why—
> "One fair daughter, and no more,
> The which he loved passing well."
>
> Polonius: Still on my daughter.
>
> Hamlet: Am I not i' th' right, old Jephthah?
>
> Polonius: If you call me Jephthah, my lord, I have a daughter that I love passing well.

Hamlet: Nay, that follows not.

Polonius: What follows then, my lord?

Hamlet: Why—
"As by lot, God wot,"
and then, you know,
"It came to pass, as most like it was"—
the first row of the pious chanson will show you more, for look
where my abridgement comes.

Enter the players.

Hamlet's reference is to a story in Judges 11 (in the Geneva Bible version), and to a then-current ballad on the subject. Jephthah promised the Lord that if he would give Jephthah victory over the Ammonites, Jephthah would offer up the first person to come out his front door as a burnt offering. His daughter and only child is the lucky winner. Before she's sacrificed, she begs leave for, and receives, permission to spend two months in the mountains with her "companions" to bewail her eternal virginity. (There's that two months again.) She gets herself to a nunnery. Then Jephthah "did with her according to his vow which he had vowed: and she had known no man."

Hamlet is chiding Polonius for similarly selling off his own daughter—barring her marriage and procreation, and ultimately sacrificing her life. And he is also jabbing an insult at Polonius (and commenting slantingly on his own situation): Jephthah was "the son of a harlot."

For those who are interested, here's the "first row," or stanza, from the chanson that Hamlet's referring to (this the most accurate rendition, reported in *The Roxburghe Ballads* of 1889 from a 1675 manuscript):

I read that many years agoe,
    when *Jepha* Judge of *Israel*
Had one fair Daughter and nore more,
    whom he loved so passing well.
And as by lot, God wot,
It came to passe, most like it was,

Great warrs there should be,
And who should be the chiefe, but he, but he.

Conception Is a Blessing

An aside for those who wonder whether Hamlet and Ophelia were lovers (physically), and for those who have the temerity to suggest that she might have been pregnant by Hamlet: There's no conclusive evidence that either of these is true. But the unending references to her virginity—or lack of same—are damned suggestive.

Suppose Ophelia conceived a child by Hamlet in the month or so preceding the November 2 court scene, when she was warned off by Polonius and Laertes. One can imagine her consoling Hamlet in his grief (during those audiences Polonius has heard about), one thing leading to another, and nature taking its course. She'd be three or four months gone and just starting to "show" at the time of her madness and suicide.

Both Laertes' and Polonius' sermons to Ophelia are all about retaining her virginity against Hamlet's importunings, and given their anxiety on this issue, one has to wonder if the horse might not be out of the barn already. Also consider Hamlet's suggestive lines to Polonius ("Let her not walk i' the sun: conception is a blessing; but not as your daughter may conceive. Friend, look to 't." 2.2.198), and the innuendo-laden interchanges between Hamlet and Ophelia in the nunnery and mousetrap scenes.

And in Ophelia's madness, there's an interchange that's perhaps revealing. Claudius, in response to her ravings, says, "Conceit upon her father." 4.5.38 She replies, "Pray let's have no words of this, but when they ask you what it means, say you this:" She then sings her St. Valentine's song about a maid who's deflowered then cast aside. If "conceit" is taken in its sense of "conception"—certainly valid given its usage elsewhere and the bawdy content of her ravings—she could well be saying, "I'd rather not talk about conception and fathers, please; but here's a ditty on that subject."

Compare Ophelia's lines here in the madness scene: 4.5.38

Pray let's have no words of this, but when they ask you what it means, say you this:

To her interchange with Hamlet during the mousetrap: 3.2.92

Ophelia: Will 'a tell us what this show meant?

Hamlet: Ay, or any show that you will show him. Be not you
asham'd to show, he'll not shame to tell you what it means.

Ophelia: You are naught [naughty or nothing], you are naught.

Mark the "show" and "shame" here, and the repeated "what it means."
(Wink wink.) The echoes seem too perfect, in this echo-chamber of a play,
to discard or ignore.

Another quite convincing item came from an article by Erik Rosenkrantz
Bruun in *Modern Language Quarterly* (15: 1993; thanks to Matthew Steggle
and Lisa Hopkins for pointing this out to me): all the flowers that Ophelia
passes out in her madness were used in Elizabethan medicine as abortives.
This is also in keeping with Gertrude's description of the drowning: there's a
feeling that Ophelia is in something akin to a drugged state as she settles to
her watery death.

Tenuous stuff, this (how many children had Lady Ophelia?), but much in
the text suggests it, and nothing calls it false. And the idea of the teenage
Ophelia on her own in Elsinore—her brother in Paris, her father dead at her
lover's hand, she carrying Hamlet's issue, Hamlet exiled in England, and
Claudius on the throne—imparts a personal and political tension that's the
very stuff of drama. It certainly explains her teenage suicide. It also explains
why her madness does not arise until six weeks after the nunnery scene and
her father's death.

And if you really want to turn up the tension, imagine Gertrude is also
pregnant, by Claudius (it's been four or five months since their marriage).
Ophelia and Gertrude, carrying rival heirs. One might find reason therein
for Getrude's failure to intervene in Ophelia's suicide, which she seems to
have witnessed.

Oh, Wonderful Son

In her madness, Ophelia's first resort is (foolishly?) to Gertrude: "Where is
the beauteous majesty of Denmark?" 4.5.25 It's hard to think who else she
would turn to. Throughout the play, Gertrude seems to only pay attention to
the personal; she gives the impression of being blithely oblivious to the political currents swirling around her.

There's a revealing contrast, for instance, between the words of Gertrude, Claudius, and Polonius regarding Hamlet's madness. Polonius, somewhat naïve in his dotage, propounds his theory of love-madness throughout. Claudius entertains that theory, and agrees to try it by spying, but he quickly turns to a more suspicious stance.

For her part, Gertrude states the situation for what it is, seemingly unaware of the political tensions attached: "I doubt it is no other but the main,/His father's death and our [F1: o'er]hasty marriage." 2.2.62

Contrast Claudius' explanation just prior to this, shaking his head in innocent bewilderment to Rosencrantz and Guildenstern: 2.2.9

> ...What it should be,
> More than his father's death, that thus hath put him
> So much from th' understanding of himself,
> I cannot dream of.

From her appeal to Hamlet not to leave for Wittenberg right up through the swordfight scene, and including even her hasty marriage to Claudius, Gertrude seems unaware of the political import of her words and actions. I'm not the first to note that as a dramatic character, Gertrude is largely inert.

But there's one huge exception to that inertia, where this shallow character is forced to face depths—the closet scene with Hamlet after the mousetrap. And the power of that scene is for me perhaps the strongest argument for a youthful Hamlet. If Hamlet is a teen, the closet scene rises from an Oedipal implausibility (Gibson and Close, Branagh and Christie, et al.) to a tour de force that has no equal in any other play, or any other playwright, that I know of.

Hamlet enters her chamber at Gertrude's behest (per Polonius and Claudius' plotting), following the mousetrap scene: 3.4.12

> Hamlet: Now, mother, what's the matter?
>
> Queen: Hamlet, thou hast thy father much offended.
>
> Hamlet: Mother, you have my father much offended.

Queen: Come, come, you answer with an idle tongue.

Hamlet: Go, go, you question with a wicked tongue.

So the scene begins with a smart-ass, rebellious, teenage son—with the annoying if justified peevishness of children from broken homes—arguing with his mother. Mothers, sons, does this ring true for an adult son?

Within half a dozen lines, Gertrude is ready to leave and pass him off: "Nay, then I'll set those to you that can speak." 3.4.24 (i.e. "Just wait until your father gets home!") But Hamlet doesn't allow it, and turns her to the mirror.

The interchange that follows—with Hamlet alternately pleading, cajoling, and browbeating, and Gertrude steadily abandoning her defenses—is a thing of beauty when you view Hamlet as an ardent youth and Gertrude as a young woman. And Gertrude's capitulation to her boy ("O Hamlet, speak no more!/Thou turn'st my eyes into my very soul," 3.4.99 and "O Hamlet, thou hast cleft my heart in twain." 3.4.176) achieves a poignancy that is tepid with an adult son. "O wonderful son, that can so stonish a mother!" 3.2.244

Add that Gertrude is the potential mother of a competing heir, and Hamlet's imperative "go not to my uncle's bed" 3.4.179 takes on political shades that off-color his obvious personal motives.

The Imperial Jointress of this War-Like State

In the discussion above I've spoken of Gertrude as blithely ignorant, even inert, in the swirl of Danish politics. The only time she appears to engage in palace intrigue is when she agrees, in her closet, to conceal Hamlet's sanity from Claudius (and her ensuing adherence to that promise). But many have noticed that Gertrude's inconsequential character is odd in this play where every action, and every character, has consequences. Perhaps there's another view of Gertrude that's quite the opposite—a view that is evidenced, ironically, by the very lack of any evidence to support it.

In a brilliant series of articles on *Hamlet* and Elizabethan inheritance law in *Shakespeare Newsletter* (Fall and Winter 2000/2001), Anthony Burton has shown that by marrying Claudius within a month, Gertrude effectively disinherits Hamlet. His birthright becomes the property of Claudius, as Gertrude's husband. And if Claudius has an heir, Hamlet is disinherited forever. This was not arcane knowledge, especially among the courtiers and Inns of Court lawyers who were among Shakespeare's best customers. And the inheritance issues of younger sons like Claudius were a common trope in the drama of the day—think of Orlando in *As You Like It*.

As Burton demonstrates, the language of inheritance pervades the play. The gravedigger's legal quibbles are the most obvious examples, but think also—for just one other example—of Laertes' warning to Ophelia regarding Hamlet: "his will is not his own." 1.3.17

> Perhaps he loves you now,
> And now no soil or cautel doth besmirch
> The virtue of his will, but you must fear
>
> ...
>
> He may not, as unvalued persons do,
> Carve for himself

"Cautel" means deceit or trickery, and "carve" was a common legalism referring to heirs "carving out"—taking—their own inheritance without the approval of the executor. It's Claudius's (and Gertrude's) trickeries that besmirch Hamlet's "will,", and prevent him from carving out his legacy—a legacy he might have hoped to share with Ophelia. Laertes and Polonius have chosen rather to accede to Claudius' will.

Gertrude maintains her own personal, political, and financial position while disinheriting, displacing, and marginalizing (and arguably endangering) her own son. That behavior is not unusual in royal politics; Alexander's female progenitors were guilty of far worse crimes against their sons, including and even especially against their eldest sons—including murder for reasons of succession. But it's not in keeping with the generally held view of a Gertrude who is unconscious and largely ineffectual.

Consider Gertrude's position on King Hamlet's death: a young woman facing decades as dowager queen—an inessential appendix to the body politic, perhaps never to marry, with her son as her lord and keeper. (Though according to Burton she would have retained a third of her husband's for tune in any case.) By marrying Claudius, she retains her preeminent position in court and country, and that as wife to a charming and consumate young king who—to put it in modern terms—knows how to party.

If Gertrude's decision to marry was so calculated, then her apparent lack of calculation throughout the play makes her the most sophisticated manipulator in the drama. Her blithe and bald comment on Hamlet's distem-

per—"I doubt it is no other but the main;/His father's death, and our
o'erhasty marriage"—reveals a cold, clear-eyed, and dispassionate view of
the state of things that would merit a look of no little surprise and admira-
tion from Claudius, whose craft is so much more overt.

This is only one view of Gertrude—far different from the queen we've
always known. But it's a view that aligns with everything else we know about
the intrigues larding the Danish court.

There's no evidence that Gertrude knew of the murder, either before or
after the event—in fact even at the end of the play (see Chapter Five). Nor,
despite much speculation by the critics, is there any evidence of her adultery
before King Hamlet's death. But when the situation arose, it didn't take
Gertrude long to emerge from it, and in remarkably good condition and
position. She definitely lands on her feet.

The Morn and Liquid Dew of Youth

If you view Hamlet as a teen, and those around him (especially Gertrude) as
young, the political and personal relationships between those characters
make sense in a way that they simply don't if Hamlet is thirty. Gertrude's
ability to bear a rival heir, Claudius' need to cement his power and dynasty,
the roles of Polonius, Laertes, and poor Ophelia in the political power struggle, Hamlet's innuendos, quibbles, jibes, and barbs, all these things cohere
into a consistent sense and sensibility—one that's rife with personal, political, and especially dramatic tensions—which falls apart with an older protagonist.

The picture that emerges of a court embroiled in a thinly veiled family
succession struggle mirrors the ongoing tensions in the courts of Elizabeth
and her predecessors. In 1601, after 43 years of uninterrupted (if often troubled) rule, Elizabeth's courtiers were already anticipating and maneuvering
in preparation for the accession (perhaps) of James of Scotland, with his wife
Anne of Denmark. Given that atmosphere of the times, and of times past,
you can see in the play a carefully indirect reflection of the English court
since time immemorial—a reflection that Shakespeare had shown his audience repeatedly over the preceding decade through his history plays. Will's
auditors and readers would have understood that Italianate political context
almost viscerally; it would have imbued the play with whole layers of dramatic tension, power, and effect.

In the next chapter I take a closer look at the relationship between *Hamlet* and some events of the day—particularly those in which Shakespeare was personally involved—and what those relationships tell us about this young prince and those around him.

CHAPTER FOUR

The Age Is Grown So Pick'd

Many critics have noted that *Hamlet* is the Shakespeare play most laden with topical references and allusions (though Shakespeare is ever elusive this way)—to people and events at court, to plays at the public and private theaters, to poets, courtiers, and perhaps even one tavernkeeper. There are dozens of in-jokes—some of them remarkably involved—littering the play.

Like his brilliant young protagonist, though, Shakespeare is too savvy to make those allusions direct and obvious (and actionable). All the references and parallels are slanting and oblique, never dropping to the heavy-handed crudity of direct satire and parody. As a result, there have been centuries of controversy over what these allusions mean—whether Hamlet's words to the players are Shakespeare's comments on rival players and playwrights, whether Polonius is an intentional burlesque of Elizabeth's Secretary of State Burghley, whether Yorick is a representation of the famous clown Tarleton, and many others. It's one of those apparent allusions that's the springboard for this chapter.

The Heel of the Courtier

Even after sorting out the clown's quiddities, there's yet another blatant reference to years and durations in the graveyard scene that I haven't mentioned yet—by Hamlet, right in the thick of the other matters. Commenting on the gravedigger's saucy replies, Hamlet complains: 5.1.56, Q1: 3330

> "By the Lord, Horatio, this three [Q1: seven] years I have took note of it: the age is grown so pick'd [refined] that the toe of the peasant comes so near the heel of the courtier, he galls his kibe [rubs his blister or chilblain]. How long hast thou been grave-maker?"

I include the last sentence to show the proximity to the other date references ("sixteene here: man and boy, thirty years."). Given how self-consciously Shakespeare seems to use all the year references throughout the play, and especially in the graveyard scene, I couldn't help wondering what he was trying to do with this one.

Nothing is mentioned in the play that seems to have happened three or seven years prior, and the line just reeks of a topical allusion, so I assumed the reference was to some contemporary event, quite possibly one that had been lost in history. The trope of upstarts challenging the position of courtiers was a constant in Elizabethan life and literature; it was a time of widespread and newfound social mobility. (Shakespeare's Globe was one of the more turbulent cauldrons for that mixing.) But many events in Shakespeare's life put him in the thick of that roil of social classes. In particular, those events arose three and seven years prior to the graveyard scene (circa 1597/8 and 1593/4).

One item comes from the official documents we have relating to Shakespeare's life. Will's father John received a grant of arms in 1596 or 1597, allowing him and his son to sign themselves "gentleman," and elevating them a large step above their existing social state (John's father and brother— Will's grandfather and uncle—were both yeoman farmers, and John himself was repeatedly referred to as a yeoman). Will's success and available cash (and perhaps his connections in the aristocracy) probably played a role in this grant's approval, but the key hereditary rationalization for the grant was John's being married to Mary Arden, whose father was a gentleman, and whose family could be construed to have an aristocratic lineage.

Shortly after this grant, John applied to have his arms "impaled" with Mary's, adding the Arden imprimatur to the Shakespeares' status. A grant for that impalement was drawn up in 1599 (though it's unclear if the final grant was ever issued). It's tempting to see the "galls his kibe" line as Shakespeare's tossed-off quip at his own elevation, and the inevitable comments that ensued. The 1597 grant was actually challenged, formally but unsuccessfully, in 1602, citing "mean" individuals and mentioning "Shakespeare the player"—an undisguised mock. And the motto accompanying the arms, at least, had been ridiculed less formally—and more personally—prior to that.

That motto, written above Shakespeare's arms in the draft grants that are extant, perhaps best summarizes the somewhat defensive sense of the situation; it was *non sanz droict*—"not without right." Ben Jonson ridiculed the motto in his *Every Man Out of His Humour*, one of the plays in the War of the Theaters, played by Will's company in 1599 and discussed in Appendix B. Commenting on Sogliardo's newly purchased coat of arms, Puntarvolo says, "Let the word [i.e. motto] bee, Not without mustard." To add further irony, the motto was written in the preliminary draft grant—twice—with an extraneous comma: "Non, sanz droict."

1597 is also the year in which Shakespeare bought New Place—the second-best house in Stratford.

This possible self reference in the "galls his kibe" line to Shakespeare's own rising status is alluring. But if you follow Q1 and look back seven years, to 1593/94, you find the most significant event in Will's professional life—his enrollment as a leading sharer in the newly re-formed Lord Chamberlain's Men, the company with which he was associated until his death. When you look at that event in light of his reception by the literary community, a reference to overweening peasants makes a lot of sense.

As I explain in Chapter One (with more detail in Appendix A), Q1 is a bad re-creation of the play drawn from an actor's memory, so it has pretty limited authority in disputes with F1 and Q2. But even if it's false fire, Q1's "seven years" put me on the trail of Shakespeare the rising star, and that trail led me to an understanding of young Hamlet that I never expected to find in such an innocuous and offhanded (if oddly obtrusive) reference.

The Lord Chamberlain's Men

Shakespeare entered the London literary and theater scene sometime in the mid to late 1580s. The years 1585 to 1594 were tumultuous ones, with companies of players shifting, merging, disbanding, and re-combining. That tumult reached its peak during the two years June 1592 to June 1594, when the theaters were closed due to plague. Players, playwrights, and producers scrambled to make a living as they could—traveling the inn circuit in the provinces, turning out the more-publishable romantic and epic narrative poems, providing material for the nobility, and other such.

Shakespeare wrote two narrative poems during this period: *Venus and Adonis*, published in April 1593, and *The Rape of Lucrece*, published May 1594. These were by far his bestselling works during his lifetime (each went through multiple editions); they were far more influential in establishing his early literary reputation than any of the plays he had written. The first was dedicated quite formally to Henry Wriothesley, Earl of Southampton, as was the second, but more warmly and familiarly. To many, this suggests that the first dedication resulted in the kind of patronage that he might have hoped for, both personal and pecuniary. The second dedication presumably re-sulted in similar outcome.

Even so, when Nicholas Rowe tells us on questionable third-hand author-ity that Southampton gave Shakespeare 1,000 pounds, we have to take it with a seasoning of salt:

> "He had the Honour to meet with many great and uncommon
> Marks of Favour and Friendship from the Earl of *Southampton* . . . .
> There is one Instance so singular in the Magnificence of this Pa-
> tron of *Shakespear's*, that if I had not been assur'd that the Story
> was handed down by Sir *William D'Avenant*, who was probably
> very well acquainted with his Affairs, I should not have ventur'd to
> have inserted, that my Lord *Southampton*, at one time, gave him a
> thousand Pounds, to enable him to go through with a Purchase
> which he heard he had a mind to." —From the introduction and
> Shakespeare biography in Rowe's 1709 edition of the plays.

Even Rowe has trouble believing this exorbitant thousand-pound figure (despite his misplaced faith in D'Avenant), and no modern scholar that I've read gives it much credence. Some have suggested that Southampton's gift—whatever the amount—is what allowed Shakespeare to buy his one-tenth share in The Chamberlain's Men. (See the end of the chapter for another speculation on this gift.) And while it's perhaps insignificant, Dover Wilson points out that two days after Southampton achieved majority—and his full fortune—on October 6, 1594, we find the recently re-established Chamber-lain's Men in possession of the Cross Keys Inn as their winter theater, and their patron Lord Hunsdon writing to the mayor of London to "require & pray" that he give permission for them to play there. Perhaps, Wilson surmises, Southampton's generosity and/or influence allowed them to take up those quarters.

The Chamberlain's Men were chosen to present two of the five plays before the Queen that Christmas season of 1594/95 (Shakespeare, along with Richard Burbage and William Kemp, is recorded as receiving payment for those performances the following March). And for the next two decades—at least until Shakespeare's death—the company dominated the Christmas-season revels performances at court. It's not surprising, as the company was in an especially privileged position. The Master of the Revels, who was responsible for bringing plays before the queen, worked directly for their patron, the Lord Chamberlain.

These performances at court played an incredibly important role in the fabric of Elizabethan theater. The public theater was tolerated in an increasingly Puritan London only because it had the Queen's protection. Ever frugal, Elizabeth had no interest in providing sole subsidy for the plays she and her courtiers so much enjoyed, and public playing provided necessary sustenance for the acting companies that performed at court. This protection actually increased under James; Will's company became The King's Men on James' accession in 1603. The leading partners, including Shakespeare, were made Grooms of the King's Chamber—actual titled courtiers, if somewhat lowly ones.

So whatever the source of Will's share in the company, by 1594 he was a leading partner in the leading dramatic company in London—the favored company of the Queen herself. In terms of social status, starting in late 1594—seven years before Hamlet's "galls his kibe" toss-off—the still-ungentrified Will Shakespeare and his fellows were in company of courtiers; they were circulating among the leading nobility of the realm. (In an age of courtly opulence, clothes very much made the man; the players' extensive and expensive costume locker went a long way toward helping them fit in to courtly circles.)

The only item that I've found suggesting that Shakespeare actually rubbed shoulders with the aristocracy is an 1865 historian's report of an alleged letter from 1603, a letter the historian never actually saw. It's from Mary Herbert, Lady Pembroke (an important patron of and contributor to Elizabethan poetry), to one of her two sons (the First Folio was dedicated to both of them), "telling him to bring James I from Salisbury to see *As You Like It;* 'we have the man Shakespeare with us'." Thin pickings, but alluring; it's easy to imagine Will's brilliant wit being quite a draw in aristocratic salons.

We know that Richard Burbage was at least thought of fondly by at least one of the Pembrokes. Two months after Burbage's death in 1619, the third Earl, William (one of the two sons mentioned above) wrote that he could not bear to watch the company perform "so soon after the loss of my old acquaintance Burbage." And other contemporary dramatists of lowly origins— Ben Jonson for instance, who served a stint as a bricklayer and another as a common soldier—had widespread connections in the upper classes.

In *Return to Parnassus, Part II* (1601/2), quoted at more length below, two of Shakespeare's fellow players, Richard Burbage and Will Kempe, are presented as characters. Burbage says, "for honor, who of more report than Dick Burbage & Will Kempe? He's not counted a Gentleman that knows not Dick Burbage and Will Kemp." This line is ridiculing Burbage's pretensions, but that very ridicule highlights the players' rising position in society, and the resulting resentment by those of better breeding, education, wealth, and position. (The irony and contempt is extra deep here because the playwright actually figures them on stage by their own names—something no Elizabethan playwright would have dared with men of standing.)

At the very least, we know that from at least 1594 and for nearly two decades, Shakespeare spent a lot of time in the same room with Elizabeth's courtiers—though perhaps always separated by the front of the stage. And we know from various references to him and his company during this period that several of his coevals were resentful of his sudden literary and social distinction.

Shakespeare and The University Wits

The adjectives most often used of Shakespeare by his contemporaries are "honest," "sweet," and "gentle." He was remarkable for his day and profession, in that he almost never got into professional fights and contentions. Ben Jonson killed a fellow actor, Gabriel Spencer, in a duel. "Kit" Marlowe died, stabbed in the eye, in a tavern fight over the bill (though many suggest deeper spookery). Almost every major literary figure was involved in hot-blooded battles of the pen, at least, and battles at the bar and in body were common. The Elizabethan age, and the Elizabethan stage, were remarkably contentious by modern standards.

Shakespeare's squabbles—the ones we know of, at least—were few, and not very acrimonious. But they did arise. And in particular, they arose during the period 1592 to 1594. The Cambridge- and Oxford-educated writers took umbrage at this middle-class interloper whose work—both the poems and the tawdry popularized pulp for the stage—was being so well received, and so well rewarded.

The attacks on Shakespeare might actually have begun as early as 1589—and in reference to the *Ur-Hamlet*. Playwright Thomas Nashe, in his 1589 preface to fellow-playwright Robert Greene's *Menaphon*, assaulted that early *Hamlet* and its creator directly:

> "It is a common practise now a daies amongst a sort of shifting companions, that runne through every arte and thrive by none, to leave the trade of Noverint [scrivener or scribe] whereto they were borne, and busie themselves with the indevors of Art, that could scarcelie latinize their neck verse if they should have need;...if you entreate him faire in a frostie morning, he will afford you whole Hamlets, I should say handfulls of tragical speaches."

An irresistible aside: "Neck verse" refers to the practice whereby the literate could avoid execution (save their necks) in capital cases, claiming the benefit of clergy and remitting their case to ecclesiastical court, where there was no capital punishment. They were asked to read a Latin verse before the court to prove their literacy. (Typically from Psalm 51, "Have mercy upon me, O God, according to Thy loving kindness: according unto the multitude of Thy tender mercies blot out my transgressions.") Ben Jonson avoided execution this way in his trial for the duel with Gabriel Spencer. The educated upper classes had no few legal and ecclesiastical advantages, like Ophelia receiving rites even though she was a suicide ("great command o'ersways the order" 5.1.106), or Hamlet going scot-free after his murder of Polonius. Nashe's reference to neck verse associates the "shifting companions" parading as poets with criminals, and suggests they can't claim even the meanest of educations.

Whether or not Nashe is referring to Shakespeare's play (it depends on who you think wrote the *Ur-Hamlet*), this passage encapsulates the disdain that the "university wits" like Greene and Nashe held for their perceived inferiors. The trope of yeoman farmers sending their cloddish sons to town was commonplace on the Elizabethan comedic stage, and Shakespeare—the nephew and grandson of Warwickshire farmers—certainly fit that mold.

These playwrights condemned Shakespeare's type of plays for their failure to conform to the neo-Aristotelian "unities" of time, place, and action, and their bawdy language and behavior. (As demonstrated in Chapter Two, Will achieved his own "unity of time," one that makes paltry these pedants' simplistic notions.) They also bemoaned the crass display of carnage so common on the popular stage. Such matters, in their opinion, should be left for indirect report in narrative verse, in the Senecan tradition. *Hamlet*'s Hecuba speech is a prime example of that genre, discussed in more detail below.

These wits' disdain for popular drama as a literary form was compounded by the disgraceful need of no few of them to make their living by writing work-for-hire for the stage, from which the players' companies earned a good income. (A playwright only got five or ten pounds for all rights to a play—two to four thousand 2002 US dollars, give or take.)

Three years later, in 1592, that same Robert Greene, who boasted Master's of Arts degrees from both Cambridge and Oxford, launched his own volley in the posthumously published *Greenes, Groats-worth of witte*. (This is the first known, definite reference to Shakespeare and theater.) Addressing his fellow university-educated writers "that spend their wits in making plaies," he complains of:

> "...those Puppets (I meane) that spake from our mouths, those Anticks garnisht in our colors.... for there is an upstart Crow, beautified with our feathers, that with his Tygers hart wrapt in a Players hyde, supposes he is as well able to bombast out a blanke verse as the best of you...is in his owne conceit the onely Shake-scene in a countrey.... let those Apes imitate your past excellence...it is pittie men of such rare wits, should be subject to the pleasure of such rude groomes."

"Shake-scene" is a clear reference to Shakespeare, and to his role as a player who gets the glory—and cash—from these playwrights' scripts. (This conveniently ignores the fact that Will was already a major contributor to the script locker.) "Tygers hart" parodies the line from Shakespeare's then-popular 3 Henry VI: "O tiger's heart wrapp'd in a woman's hide!" And—I hesitate to cite it—the reference to "rude grooms" just might support the anonymous, many-voices-removed 1748 assertion that Shakespeare began his career holding horses outside the theater.

When Greene then continues with his truculence, railing against "such peasants," it's hard not to think of Hamlet's "toe of the peasant" galling the courtier's heel.

Perhaps Shakespeare or his friends replied, because Henry Chettle, who had published Greene's pamphlet, apologized obliquely to Shakespeare later that year in an epistle to his own pamphlet, *Kind-Hartes Dream:*

> "...a letter written to diverse play-makers, is offensively by one or two of them taken,...With neither of them that take offence was I acquainted, and with one of them [Marlowe, a churlish character] I care not if I never be: The other...because my selfe have seene his demeanor no lesse civill than he exellent in the qualitie he professes: Besides, divers of worship have reported, his uprightness of dealing, which argues his honesty, and his facetious grace in writing, that approoves his Art."

Greene's glancing assertion of plagiarism is also referred to in a 1594 pamphlet, *Greene's Funeralls,* by "R. B.":

> Greene is the ground of everie painters die;
> Greene gave the ground to all that wrote upon him.
> Nay, more, the men that so eclipst his fame,
> Purloynde his plumes: can they deny the same?

"Purloynde his plumes" is a clear evocation of Greene's "beautified with our feathers." It's not aimed directly at Shakespeare, but it refers to the earlier passage which certainly did.

The Parnassus Plays

The attacks on Shakespeare and the Chamberlain's company by university playwrights continued up to the time *Hamlet* was written and produced. Shakespeare and his fellow players are repeatedly treated by name, both directly and obliquely, in a trilogy of plays—*The Pilgrimage to Parnassus* and *The Return to Parnassus*, Parts 1 and 2—written and put on at St. John's College, Cambridge, during the three Christmas seasons 1599/1600 to 1601/02. (See Appendix B for more on these plays.)

The trilogy's dominant, insistent (and somewhat tiring) theme is the penury and poverty to which scholars are reduced after leaving university— the ill return they receive for their wits compared to both upstart commoners and ill-educated aristocrats. One lead character is Ingenioso, a thinly disguised representation of Thomas Nashe, who graduated St. John's in 1586, left in 1588, and launched a career of polemic and invective that included the 1589 assault on the *Ur-Hamlet*'s creator cited above. Ingenioso is shown repeatedly as a sycophant resentfully pandering to stupid and niggardly aristocratic patrons, with constant sneering asides demonstrating his superior wit. There's a strong element of envy in these passages against poets who, presumably like Shakespeare with his patron Southampton, were able to receive patronage for their writings.

In *Return Part I*, a character named Gullio, "an avowed fool" and a parody of ill-educated aristocratic patrons (and of course an Oxford man), waxes *ad nauseum* to Ingenioso on Shakespeare's merits:

> Let this duncified worlde esteeme of Spencer and Chaucer, Ile worshipp sweet Mr. Shakespeare, and to honure him will lay his Venus, and Adonis under my pillow, as wee reade of one (I do not well remember his name but I am sure he was a kinge), slept with Homer under his beds heade.

Absolutely *everyone*, of course, knows that it's Alexander who kept *The Iliad* under his pillow. Gullio is here cast as the lead dunce in his own "duncified world," and his judgments on Shakespeare's work—which he values more highly than the then-nearly-deified Spencer and Chaucer—are thus ridiculed.

And in *Return, Part Two*, the lead characters, the itinerant and indigent graduates Studioso and Philomusus, are reduced to auditioning for player's work before Shakespeare's compatriots Burbage and Kemp (penultimate to their final declension into wandering fiddlers, then shepherds). Before the scholars arrive, Burbage and Kempe are parodied as they make fun of university playwrights (an especially funny piece of semi-self-ridicule in a script written by a Cambridge playwright):

> Burbage: "Now, Will Kempe, if we can intertaine these scholars at a low rate [hire them cheap], it will be well, they have oftentimes a good conceit in a part.
>
> Kempe: It's true indeed, honest Dick, but the slaves are somewhat proud, and besides, tis good sporte in a part to see them...
>
> Burbage: A little teaching will mend these faults, and it may be besides they will be able to pen a part.
>
> Kempe: Few of the university men pen plays well, they smell too much of that writer Ovid, and that writer Metamorphosis, and talk too much of Proserpina and Jupiter. Why here's our fellow Shakespeare puts them all down, ay and Ben Jonson too. And that Ben Jonson is a pestilent fellow, he brought up Horace giving the Poets a pill, but our fellow Shakespere hath given him a purge that made him beray his credit.

Kemp (who was, indeed, a clownish comedian of the old school, though a quite literate one) is ridiculed here for not knowing that Ovid is the author of *The Metamorphoses.* And he contrasts Shakespeare to both the university men and to Ben Jonson. Jonson was raised a bricklayer—not a university man except perhaps very briefly—but he was a great promoter of the classical virtues in theater that the university playwrights championed. For more on *Parnassus*'s Ben Jonson and Shakespeare comments, see Appendix B.

Again, a note of resentment runs through this *Parnassus* passage against the players who make a good living, and gain social distinction, as a result of university writers' scripts. Says Burbage to the boys:

> "But be merry my lads, you have happened upon the most excellent vocation in the world: for money, they come North and South to bring it to our playhouse, and for honor, who of more report than Dick Burbage & Will Kempe? He's not counted a Gentleman that knows not Dick Burbage and Will Kemp."

Philomusus doesn't express their position so sanguinely: "Must the basest trade yield us relief?/Must we be practis'd [apprenticed] to those leaden spouts?"

The financial situation for Elizabethan poets is perhaps best encapsulated in Francis Meres' 1598 *Palladis Tamia.* He complains that patrons are hard to come by, but says poets will get by "if our witty comedians and stately trage-dians (the glorious and goodlie representers of fine wit, glorified phrase, and quaint action) be still supported and upheld, by which means for lack of patrons (o ungrateful and damned age) our poets are solely or chiefly main-tained, countenanced, and patronized." This situation—relying on common players for their livelihood—didn't sit well with the university poets.

To condense this decade of abuse and envy by the university wits (good-natured as some of it may have been):

> **1589.** The author of the *Ur-Hamlet* and his ilk are ridiculed as "Noverint whereto they were borne,…that could scarcelie latinize their neck verse."

> **1592.** Shakespeare is directly targeted as an "upstart Crow, beauti-fied with our feathers,…supposes he is as well able to bombast out a blanke verse as the best of you."

> **1593.** Shakespeare publishes the wildly successful *Venus and Adonis,* dedicated to the Earl of Southampton.

> **1594.** The "upstart crow" assault is echoed in another pamphlet. Shakespeare publishes *The Rape of Lucrece* (also dedicated to Southampton), helps to organize and becomes the resident play-wright, partner, and a leading actor in the Lord Chamberlain's men. The company plays before the Queen at Christmas that year, and dominates the revels in every year ensuing.

> **Christmas 1601/1602.** Shakespeare and his cohorts are parodied as overweening upstarts in the third play of a three-year trilogy by students at St. John's College, Cambridge.

So when Hamlet complains to Horatio about all the social climbers over the last seven years, Shakespeare is casting his hero as the very type that had repeatedly attacked Shakespeare's own rising prominence. The most pointed attacks were in 1592–1594, seven or eight years before *Hamlet*. Those were the years when Shakespeare published his most highbrow, bestselling, and only patronized works, and when he helped to form the Chamberlain's Men, thereby becoming the leading playwright to the queen herself.

Hamlet the Player

When I started looking at Hamlet as a somewhat snobbish aristocratic university blood, much about his words and actions came clear, especially regarding the players. When he first encounters them, for instance, he begs a speech of the first player, a speech that is Senecan to the core—old-fashioned narrative verse reporting, not showing, lofty and bloody deeds of the Greeks and Trojans. (The actors here are playing characters—Hamlet and the First Player—who are themselves actors speaking in the role of Aeneas, and he is reporting to Dido the drama that transpired in Troy. We're deep in Plato's cave here.)

Hamlet launches into a panegyric for the speech worthy of the university wits: 2.2.303

"I heard thee speak me a speech once, but it was never acted, or if it was, not above once; for the play, I remember, pleas'd not the million, 'twas caviary [caviar] to the general, but it was—as I receiv'd it, and others, whose judgments in such matters cried in the top of mine—an excellent play, well digested in the scenes, set down with as much modesty as cunning. I remember one said there were no sallets [seasoned passages] in the lines to make the matter savory, nor no matter in the phrase that might indict the author of affection, but call'd it an honest method, as wholesome as sweet, and by very much more handsome than fine."

For some reason even quite conservative critics have been unable to resist the idea that Hamlet's views on theater are Shakespeare's own, and the more speculative ones go even further. A. L. Rowse's execrable biography of Shakespeare is the most egregious example. Speaking of Hamlet, he says, "Everyone sees that he is the most autobiographical of all the characters."

And of *Hamlet*: "It is fullest of what Shakespeare himself thought of the theater." Likewise Katherine Duncan-Jones in her wonderfully insightful but decidedly uneven *Ungentle Shakespeare* (1991): "As for Shakespeare: we may clearly view the scenes with the players in *Hamlet* as broadly personal. It also seems quite reasonable to see Hamlet's extended advice to the Player, which opens 3.2, as an expression of his own views on acting technique."

But listen to Hamlet's words. The play was written with "as much modesty as cunning"? "No sallets [seasoning] in the lines to make the matter savory?" "Nor matter in the phrase"? "As wholesome as sweet"? "More handsome than fine"? It's completely beyond me how anyone can view this "caviary to the general" passage as anything but a parody of Hamlet and his elitist playgoing friends ("others, whose judgments in such matters cried in the top of mine") espousing their views on playwriting—a parody written by an unfailingly populist playwright.

The scenes with the players also tell us more about Hamlet. We know from his "I heard thee speak me a speech once, but it was never acted" 2.2.303 that he's more than just another spectator; he has private time with the players. His welcome to them reinforces that notion. To the First Player: "Welcome, good friends. O, old friend! why, thy face is valanc'd [bearded] since I saw thee last." 2.2.301 (He refers to him again as "old friend" later in the scene 2.2.537, and to the other players as "friends.") And to the boy who plays the women's parts: "Thy ladyship is nearer to heaven than when I saw you last by the altitude of a chopine [elevator shoe, often used by boy players and by players in inn-yards or at fairs, lacking a raised platform on which to perform]." So for what it's worth, it's been some months since he's seen them.

Hamlet is more like a patron, in the mold of the Earl of Southampton or the Pembrokes (or *Parnassus'* supercilious Gullio?), than an auditor. He commissions the troupe to play before the court, and browbeats Polonius into giving them good hospitality. But he's also a wannabe amateur play wright and actor. He's the first to launch into a speech when the players arrive ("We'll e'en to't like French falc'ners: fly at any thing we see; we'll have a speech straight." 2.2.301), and is ready to compose his "speech of some dozen lines, or sixteen lines" 2.2.377 at a moment's notice. And his extended advice on acting 3.2.3—accepted with such admirable restraint by the First Player—marks Hamlet as a know-it-all, aristocratic, teenage patron who is just the type to first- or second-guess the players, or toss gibes at the them from his privileged seat on the stage (as he in fact does).

Immediately after the King departs the mousetrap, Hamlet sings a ditty to Horatio, and asks, "Would not this, sir, and a forest of feathers—if the rest of my fortunes turn Turk with me—with two Provincial roses on my raz'd shoes, get me a fellowship in a cry of players?" 3.2.210

"Half a share," quips Horatio.

Hamlet's yen for theater makes me think of Fortinbras' closing words, in a context very different from that of the final scene: "Bear Hamlet like a soldier to the stage/For he was likely, had he been put on,/To have prov'd most royal." 5.2.347 Young Hamnet Shakespeare, had he not died so young, would have inherited a fellowship—about a tithe's share—in perhaps the greatest cry of players ever. Will might have preferred his son to live the life of a landed gentleman. But on the other hand, Hamnet might well have been wearing those chopines, had he been put on. He was likely to have proved most royal as well.

His Picture in Little

Hamlet's interplay with the players, and his condescending comment to Horatio in the graveyard, give a picture of Hamlet that we idolaters have been loath to admit. He is, among other things, an aristocratic university wit—not so different in some ways from the shallow characters of Rosencrantz, Guildenstern, and Osric that Shakespeare paints so tellingly, and the inconsiderable aristocratic patrons that the *Parnassus* playwright makes mock of. It's a picture that Elizabeth's courtiers, inns-of-court men, and university denizens of schools like St. John's, Cambridge—including Southampton, Shakespeare's probable patron—would have found very familiar.

I'm pleased to note that at least two scholars, interestingly both women and both Shakespeare biographers, have also pointed out this aspect of Hamlet's character. Marchette Chute's 1949 *Shakespeare of London* (my favorite Shakespeare biography) first planted the seeds in my mind some years ago. And Katherine Duncan-Jones perceived it as well, in her 2001 *Ungentle Shakespeare*.

While it may be no more than idle conjecture, viewing Hamlet as a noble patron in the mold of Southampton might just put the punch line to a wonderfully involved and reflexive topical joke that we haven't copped to in the past. Nicholas Rowe, relying on second- or third-hand authority and writing almost a century after Shakespeare's death, tells us that Shakespeare played the ghost. He also tells us—apparently on even more tenuous grounds—that

Southampton gave Will a thousand pounds for "a purchase he heard he had a mind to." Even if the sum is specious, perhaps there was a rumor of that amount, which rumor Shakespeare knew of and which Rowe picked up later. Some suggest that Will used it to buy his share in the Chamberlain's Men. If it was a loan, Will probably didn't have much collateral to back it up.

Now think about Hamlet's first line to Horatio after the mousetrap— about getting a "fellowship in a cry of players." And the line that follows? "I'll take the ghost's word for a thousand pound." Would Southampton have taken Will's word for the same sum?

Th' Expectation and Rose of The Fair State

Topical jokes, quibbles, allusions, and puns are irresistible. They certainly were for Shakespeare, says Samuel Johnson:

> "A quibble is to Shakespeare, what luminous vapours are to the traveller; he follows it at all adventures; it is sure to lead him out of his way, and sure to engulf him in the mire…. A quibble was to him the fatal Cleopatra for which he lost the world, and was content to lose it."

The same could be said for many of us who get hooked on Shakespeare, and for Hamlet as well. But still: Hamlet is much more than a glib, Osric-like courtier or supercilious teenage patron. He is, in Ophelia's words, "The courtier's, soldier's, scholar's, eye, tongue, sword." 3.1.133 That complexity of character is what makes him so fascinating.

And it's that greater character that comes to the fore in the remarkable scenes of the final act—the graveyard, the "interim," and the swordfight.

CHAPTER FIVE

Bear Hamlet Like a Soldier

Hamlet may have elitist views about the theater, but he's not just an effete intellectual with pretensions to the stage. We wouldn't have much truck with him if he were. He's also a prince, son to a warlike king, raised and educated to rule and lead his country in peace and war. Fortinbras' "he was likely, had he been put on,/To have prov'd most royal" 5.2.348 speaks to that directly. There's much in the play that paints Hamlet as a worthy master for his warlike state.

Looking at the tightly woven chronology laid out in Chapter Two, one thing in particular stands out for me—the six-week gap from January 7 to February 14, when Hamlet was with the pirates. Even before I'd sorted out all the dates, I always wondered what Hamlet was *doing* all that time. There's much about Hamlet and the pirates that illuminates both Hamlet the prince and *Hamlet* the play.

The Greatest Honor

My first real glimmer of understanding came as I was wandering around in the Amleth tale as told in Belleforest, Shakespeare's direct or indirect source for the play. At the very beginning of that account, Belleforest tells us:

Now the greatest honor that men of noble birth could at that time
win and obtaine, was in exercising the art of Piracie upon the seas;
assayling their neighours, & the countries bordering upon them;
and how much the more they used to rob, pill, and spoyle other
Prouinces, and Lands farr adiacent, so much the more their hon-
ours and reputation increased and augmented: wherein Horuendile [King Hamlet] obtained the highest place in his time, beeing
the most renouned Pirate that in those dayes scoured the seas.

We can see Horuendile mirrored in old Hamlet's "faire and warlike
form." 1.1.61 His exploits—overcoming Old Fortinbras in single combat,
slaying the sledded Polacks on the ice, bringing England under his dominion—all give him "the highest place in his time," make him a king of honor
in the old school.

But young Hamlet didn't come up in his father's school. He's a product of
the new thinking of Wittenberg (and Oxford and Cambridge, and the Inns
of Court). When we see Hamlet in contrast to the warlike Fortinbras, the
fiery Laertes, even Claudius, who says, "I have seen myself, and serv'd
against, the French," 4.7.91 we see a child of the "drossy age" 5.2.34—un-
schooled in battle—but with the expectations upon him imposed by the old.

As Fortinbras says, he could have lived up to those expectations, could
have proved most royal, if he'd taken his place on the throne. His encounter
with the pirates, reported in his letter to Horatio, shows his mettle: 4.6.12

"Ere we were two days old at sea, a pirate of very warlike appoint-
ment gave us chase. Finding ourselves too slow of sail, we put on a
compell'd valor, and in the grapple I boarded them. On the instant
they got clear of our ship, so I alone became their prisoner. They
have dealt with me like thieves of mercy, but they knew what they
did: I am to do a good turn for them."

Hamlet was the first and only one unto the breach. The compelled valor
he and his compatriots put on must have been vigorous for the pirates to
break off so quickly. (Though Derek Savage argues somewhat persuasively in
his 1950 *Hamlet & the pirates* that Hamlet had actually prearranged this encounter with the pirates to escape Claudius.)

Hamlet seems to have gotten along famously during his time with the pirates. They keep him with them for some weeks, deliver letters for him to Horatio, Claudius, and the Queen (though we never learn the contents of the letter to Gertrude, or the other letter to Claudius, unless they serve to "do the good turn" for the pirates that Hamlet has promised), deliver him back to Denmark, and take Horatio to meet him. When he tells Horatio in the final scene that "I have been in continual practice" at fencing 5.2.143, I can only assume that since he left Marcellus and the other officers of the guard in Denmark, he's been at practice with the pirates. That rough training does much to explain Hamlet's victory over Laertes' effete Parisian "rapier and dagger." 5.2.145

As it turns out, my description here of Hamlet's time with the pirates is remarkably similar to young Julius Caesar's thirty-eight days as a pirate captive, as reported at the beginning of the life of Caesar in Plutarch's *Lives*— one of Shakespeare's favorite sources. (I discuss the significance of those thirty-eight days in Chapter Two.) Here's the relevant passage, from the 1579 North translation that Will was so familiar with:

. . .he took to sea again, and was taken by pirates about the Isle of Pharmacusa : for those pirates kept all upon that sea-coast, with a great fleet of ships and boats. They asking him at the first twenty talents for his ransom, Caesar laughed them to scorn, as though they knew not what a man they had taken, and of himself promised them fifty talents. Then he sent his men up and down to get him this money, so that he was left in manner alone among these thieves of the Cilicians (which are the cruellest butchers in the world), with one of his friends, and two of his slaves only : and yet he made so little reckoning of them, that, when he was desirous to sleep, he sent unto them to command them to make no noise. Thus was he eight-and-thirty days among them, not kept as a prisoner, but rather waited upon by them as a prince. All this time he would boldly exercise himself in any sport or pastime they would go to. And other while he would write verses, and make orations, and call them together to say them before them : and if any of them seemed as though they had not understood him, or passed not for them, he called them blockheads and brute beasts, and, laughing, threatened them that he would hang them up. But they were as merry with the matter as could be, and took all in good part, thinking that this his bold speech came through the simplicity of his youth.

Plutarch's account gives some support for my otherwise tenuous assertion that Hamlet practiced fencing with the Danish guards, and then with the pirates. Caesar's prediliction for writing verses and making speeches, and his supercilious attitude, is also quite reminiscent of the Hamlet we find in the play, at least as I've described him in Chapter Four. And his "bold speech" which "came through the simplicity of youth" is in keeping with Hamlet's youth, his mad antics, and his feigned simple-mindedness as depicted in the traditional Amleth legend.

Shakepeare's *Julius Caesar* debuted only a year or two before *Hamlet*. And Caesar raises his head repeatedly in *Hamlet*, his ghost ringing through the play. In the opening scene, Horatio recalls the "harbingers" 1.1.122 preceding his death. Polonius tells us that he played the role at university: "I did enact Julius Caesar: I was killed i' the Capitol; Brutus killed me." 3.2.103 And Hamlet invokes him in the graveyard, in one of the blackest and most resounding couplets in the play: "Imperious Caesar, dead and turn'd to clay,/Might stop a hole to keep the wind away:" 5.1.213

As I discussed in Chapter One, both Caesar and Alexander are summoned in close proximity to the whole age business in the gravedigger scene, at least partially as examples of young princes who came to power and glory on their fathers' deaths. In Plutarch's account, Caesar was just "a boy," but already of consequence politically, when he was taken by the pirates. (He was actually about twenty-two at the time, but Will didn't know that.) Given all this, and especially given the 38-day correlation described in Chapter Two, it's not difficult to believe that Caesar's pirate escapade served as one model for Hamlet's.

The Undiscover'd Country

I go on so about the pirate voyage because it's while he's with the pirates that Hamlet changes from the antic, manic, changeable boy of the cellar, the nunnery, the mousetrap, and the closet, to the graver, more powerful character of the graveyard and the swordfight. To use Hamlet's description of Horatio, he becomes one of "those/Whose blood and judgment are so well co-meddled,/That they are not a pipe for Fortune's finger/To sound what stop she please," 3.2.31 a "man/That is not passion's slave." This echoes Hamlet's words to Gertrude just before his departure for England: "at your age/The heyday in the blood is tame, it's humble,/And waits upon the judgment." 3.4.78

After Hamlet leads men and faces death in battle with the pirates, and after he spends weeks with those pirates—men of his father's timber—he no longer speaks flippantly of the strumpet Fortune, or rails against her slings and arrows, but accedes to the powers of fate: "There's a divinity that shapes our ends,/Rough-hew them how we will." 5.2.12 "Even in that was heaven ordinant." 5.2.54 "There is special providence in the fall of a sparrow....let be." 5.2.147 Compare Hamlet's flippant "I will prophesy, he [Polonius] comes to tell me of the players" 2.2.277 to his commanding "I do prophesy th' election lights/On Fortinbras, he has my dying voice." 5.2.300 The Hamlet of that final act might take Fortinbras' words as his own: "I embrace my fortune." 5.2.338

It's in this final act that Hamlet comes to terms with his own mortality—arguably the defining change between a teen and a mature adult. This is not as major a shift as some have suggested. From the first lines of his first soliloquy he wishes for death ("O! that this too too solid flesh would melt,/Thaw and resolve itself into a dew."1.2.133). He never expresses concern about his own death except in the "To be or not to be" soliloquy. And that speech, as I explained in Chapter Three, is being played to Claudius; it's not Hamlet's true character being poured out.

But nevertheless, Hamlet achieves a greater maturity regarding death in the final act. Take, for example, his words at the graveside: 5.1.86

> Hamlet: Why may not imagination trace the noble dust of Alexander, till 'a find it stopping a bunghole?
>
> Horatio: 'Twere to consider too curiously, to consider so.
>
> Hamlet: No, faith, not a jot, but to follow him thither with modesty enough and likelihood to lead it.

The likelihood of his own death—and his acceptance of that likelihood—leads him to a modesty (moderation) with which he can follow Alexander in all his greatness. "The undiscover'd country" no longer "puzzles the will." 3.1.78 He accepts mortality, with no need for supernatural consolations. In his dying words he rings a remarkably unchristian and modern note: "The rest is silence." 5.2.358

To Act, To Do, and To Perform

It's with the pirates and in the graveyard that Hamlet resolves one of his central conflicts—which I am by no means the first to notice—his conflict between acting and "acting." He's an avid enthusiast for plays and players, but his disdain for "acting" arises throughout the play, from his very first speech: "Seems, madam? nay, it is, I know not 'seems.'/'Tis not alone my inky cloak, good mother,/Nor customary suits of solemn black,/.../...These indeed seem,/For they are actions that a man might play." 1.2.80

In Act 5, Hamlet with his "prophetic soul" 1.5.48 comes to a philosophy that's downright prescient in its foreshadowing of modern existential thought. (To borrow from Jan Kott, it's tempting to think of "Hamlet our contemporary.") Hamlet achieves a calm acceptance of the absurdity of human action in the face of that "fell sergeant, Death," 5.2.277 and accepts the fact that all actions are merely "acting." Face to face with Yorick, Gertrude's tears are no more meaningful than Hecuba's, unless thinking make them so.

This is not to say that Hamlet returns from his journey as some kind of uniformly wise and philosophic paragon. The snotty "galls his kibe" 5.1.56 line discussed in Chapter Four, and his contemptuous treatment of Osric, belie that widely held view, as does his petulant affray with Laertes in the graveyard (and perhaps in the grave itself—the play versions and not least the critics disagree on this).

Hamlet's somewhat inexplicable anger at Laertes—seemingly for nothing but his overacting (o'ertopping Pelion and tearing a passion to tatters)—and his perplexing obtuseness about why Laertes is angry at him ("What is the reason that you use me thus?/I lov'd you ever" 5.1.177) are in direct contradiction to the profound, meditative nature Hamlet displayed just moments before. When you consider his ambivalence toward "acting" and his prating advice to the players deriding overblown tragic acting, his excessive anger at Laertes (resentment, it seems, for Laertes o'ertopping Hamlet's own histrionics) is ironic in at least six different directions. Hamlet's complexity of character—and his distraction—don't end with the pirate voyage.

But he is much changed. When he's invited to the swordfight, he senses that all is not right: "thou wouldst not think how ill all's here about my heart; but it is no matter." (This echoes Francisco's words only ten lines into the opening scene—"I am sick at heart"). Horatio encourages him to listen to his heart and decline, offering to make excuse for him, but Hamlet tries to make light of it: "It is but foolery; but it is such a kind of gain-giving [misgiving] as would perhaps trouble a woman" 5.2.145 The "but" in that line makes it tempting to read this as a newfound if short-lived respect for women's wisdom, in contrast to his contemptuous behavior throughout the play.

He then gives us this final statement of his mature philosophy, for some of us the most important lines in the English language: 5.2.147

Not a whit, we defy augury. There is special providence in the fall of a sparrow. If it be now, 'tis not to come; if it be not to come, it will be now; if it be not now, yet it will come—the readiness is all. Since no man, of aught he leaves, knows what is't to leave betimes [at the right time], let be.

The last sentence is also, unfortunately, one of the most difficult textual problems in the play. The Q2 and F1 versions of the passage vary markedly, and the last sentence is missing from Q1. There are at least half a dozen valid readings of that final, resounding line; I've given my preferred. Here are the original versions in all their punctuational glory, so you can create your own:

Second Quarto Q2: 3668
Not a whit, we defie augury, there is speciall prouidence, in the fall of a Sparrowe, if it be, tis not to come, if it be not to come, it will be now, if it be not now, yet it well come, the readines is all, since no man of ought he leaues, knowes what ist to leaue betimes, let be.

First Folio F1: 3668
Not a whit, we defie Augury; there's a speciall Prouidence in the fall of a sparrow. If it be now, 'tis not to come: if it bee not to come, it will bee now: if it be not now; yet it will come; the readinesse is all, since no man ha's ought of what he leaues. What is't to leaue be-times?

First Quarto Q1: 3668

No Horatio, not I, if danger be now,/Why then it is not to come, theres a predestinate prouidence/in the fall of a sparrow.

Various critics have called Hamlet's act-five character fatalism, malaise, or just a continuation of his melancholy. But it is certainly a mature, seasoned counterpoint to his earlier character, forever buffeted by the winds southerly and north-northwest. (cf. Hamlet's "sea of troubles" 3.1.69 and Gertrude's "Mad as the sea and wind, when both contend/Which is the mightier." 4.1.9) Ironically, in his time at sea with the pirates he has found "grounds more relative"—more solid—on which to stand. 2.2.438

Hamlet, Revenge!

The notion echoed in that line—that Hamlet needs more solid grounds to justify his revenge—also gives much reason for his delay.

Hamlet is unique in a singular aspect, one I haven't seen noted by any critic. In *Hamlet,* nobody even knows that the primal murder has occurred. This is not true of any previous revenge tragedy—Elizabethan or classical— or of the Saxo and Belleforest versions of the tale. Claudius knows, of course, as do Hamlet and Horatio (though with dubious certitude). But no other character knows that King Hamlet was murdered—even (especially) at the end of the play.

This singular fact is among other things a dramatic device addressing the central problem of revenge tragedies—once the revenge happens, the play's over. The characters' ignorance is responsible for much of *Hamlet*'s dramatic force, effect…and duration. It's what drives the action of the play (or lack of same). *Hamlet* is remarkable in dramatic history for that alone; Shakespeare builds a four-hour play on this traditionally slender scaffolding. But it also encapsulates one of *Hamlet*'s central and oft-discussed themes: the tension of uncertain knowledge that pervades the castle of Elsinore—that rings from the opening line ("Who's there?") to the end of the play and beyond.

On realizing this singularity, I started looking at what I'll call "the epistemology of *Hamlet*"—who knows what, and when. In particular, I looked at what various characters know about King Hamlet's murder in the course of the play. A chronological exploration, once again, does much clarify the basic sense of what happens, and when.

Murder Most Foul

To begin with, we can assume that Claudius knows of the murder throughout the play. He admits his guilt to the audience twice, in passages I'll discuss below.

After his contretemps with the ghost, Hamlet believes—and wants to believe—that his father was murdered. But he doesn't know it. The reliability of the ghost is put in question by various characters throughout the play, including Hamlet. ("The spirit that I have seen/May be a dev'l, and the dev'l hath power/T' assume a pleasing shape." 2.2.598) The centuries of controversy about the ghost (culminating in some definitive studies by Prosser, Greenblatt, and McGee in the late twentieth century) demonstrate quite clearly that the ghost's provenance and credibility are uncertain—to Hamlet, Horatio, the officers, certainly to Gertrude, and likewise to the audience, whether Elizabethan or modern, popular or critical. Hamlet and the audience can't but give the ghost credence, but neither can they give it certain credence. So even after the ghost's revelation, only Hamlet and the audience know of the murder; and their knowledge is far from certain.

Bernardo, Marcellus, and Horatio all see the ghost, but they don't hear his revelations. It's quite possible, in fact, that Horatio and Marcellus don't even hear the ghost's repeated injunctions to "Swear!" echoing up in the cellarage scene. 1.5 Their astonishment there could be purely at Hamlet's wild 'havior in response—much like Gertrude's astonishment in her closet 3.4 when Hamlet sees and hears the ghost, but she doesn't. If so, Hamlet is the only character who ever hears the ghost speak, and it's not Marcellus and Horatio's discretion that the ghost is worried about, but Hamlet's resolve (as it turns out, with good reason).

Horatio hears of the murder from Hamlet sometime prior to the mousetrap, where Hamlet speaks of "the circumstance/Which I have told thee of my father's death." 3.2.41 But Horatio has only heard a secondhand report, of damned uncertain provenance, transmitted through an interlocutor of more-than-questionable reliability. The audience hears only a glancing reference to this report, emphasizing its tenuous nature.

We as audience get confirmation of the murder, and of Claudius' guilt, just before to the nunnery scene, when Claudius says in an aside, "How smart a lash that speech doth give my conscience.../The harlot's cheek.../Is not more ugly.../Than is my deed." 3.1.48 From this point forward, we know the murder happened and that Claudius did it.

The resulting discrepancy—between what we know and what the characters know—sets up the exquisite dramatic tensions in the mousetrap scene.

What Happens in the Mousetrap

It's in the mousetrap that the epistemology of *Hamlet* has been most misconstrued—almost universally so, in fact. The common view is that Hamlet gets proof and certain knowledge of Claudius' guilt after the Lucianus poisoning, when Claudius calls for lights. But the play of knowledge in the mousetrap scene is far more complex. For those who aren't in the know, I'll tip the nod here: you're about to hear an argument with two scholars—A. C. Bradley and J. D. Wilson (with asides by W. W. Greg)—who have been dead for sixty and thirty years, respectively, at this writing.

Wilson realized half a century ago that the courtiers don't see the *Gonzago* play as a reenactment of Old Hamlet's murder; they don't even know about the murder. When Lucianus pours poison in Gonzago's ear, Hamlet has just announced that Lucianus is Gonzago's nephew. So what the courtiers see is the nephew to the king poisoning the king and taking his crown. This is in a play put on by the nephew of the current king, who only three months back preempted the nephew's succession and inheritance, and arguably whored his mother.

To everyone except Claudius, Hamlet, and Horatio, the Gonzago play looks like a not terribly well-veiled threat against the king's life and crown. No wonder everyone's in such a tizzy. Rosencrantz and Guildenstern, Osric, Voltemand, Cornelius, et. al. must be feeling damned uncomfortable sitting in on this increasingly nasty family squabble. Mighty opposites and all that.

Curiously, the critics have failed to realize that Wilson's insight—so obvious once he came upon it—also answers one of their most vexing questions, about the dumb show: Why is it there? Claudius is shown the poisoning twice. Why doesn't he react the first time?

The dumb show's dramatic purpose is perhaps fairly simple, and not far to find: It reveals to Claudius that Hamlet knows of the murder. That knowledge ratchets up the dramatic tension of this scene—and the rest of the play—by an order of magnitude; knowing that Hamlet knows, Claudius sees all the prince's sneering commentary and asides for what they are—veiled innuendo dripping with threat. And Claudius' supposedly innocent question about the Gonzago play—"Have you heard the argument? Is there no of-fence in 't?" 3.2.181—takes on a far more poisonous aspect.

But why doesn't Claudius react to the dumb show? We can put aside Wil-son's idea that Claudius is in hugger-mugger conversation with Gertrude and Polonius during the dumb show, and isn't watching; it's just implausible, and has no support in the text. We can also dispense with the suggestions that have been derided as the "second tooth" theory: that Claudius could bear it when one tooth was pulled, but the second was too much for him.

But there is an obvious answer: if Claudius reacted to the dumb show, it would confirm his guilt to Hamlet (and raise the courtiers' eyebrows in cu-riosity, at least). Claudius is far too consumate to react at that point. Once Hamlet names Lucianus as nephew, though, turning the play into a threat against the king's life, Claudius' reaction—fury, not guilt—is perfectly justi-fied by anyone's lights.

And Hamlet knows that. Far from proving his guilt, Hamlet knows that Claudius could just as well be furious at the obvious threat against his life, played before the whole court. Or he could be reacting to both; Hamlet doesn't know. He wants to believe, of course, but considering the above, "I'll take the ghost's word for a thousand pound" sounds more like self-convincing than conviction.

Horatio's non-response is hardly resounding in its support: 3.2.286

> Hamlet: O good Horatio! I'll take the ghost's word for a thousand pound. Didst perceive?
>
> Horatio: Very well, my lord.
>
> Hamlet: Upon the talk of the poisoning?
>
> Horatio: I did very well note him.

Consider what's going through Horatio's mind at this moment: "Yes, I saw you put on a play before the court threatening the king's life, with you as chorus, and he got really angry in response. Yeah, I saw that." His is not a ringing endorsement.

So who learns what in the course of the mousetrap?

- The courtiers learn nothing, except that Hamlet's really upset—about being displaced, about Ophelia jilting him, and about the marriage.

- Hamlet learns nothing from either show. Claudius doesn't react to the dumb show. (Perhaps he reacts with raising of the eyebrows, or rearing back, or some such ambiguous giving out. A veiled glare at Hamlet would be good staging, so the audience knows that Claudius knows that Hamlet knows.) And when Claudius responds with such anger to *Gonzago*, Hamlet and Horatio both know there's a perfectly reasonable explanation besides guilt.

- From the moment of the dumb show poisoning, Claudius knows that Hamlet knows of the murder, and in detail; it's only emphasized by *Gonzago*. But Claudius also knows that Hamlet has no proof; if he did, he wouldn't have needed the mousetrap.

This last point is, I think, crucial—once Claudius knows that Hamlet knows, the whole dynamic of the play is changed. And I don't think it's a coincidence that the dumb-show poison lands in the king's ear almost exactly halfway through *Hamlet*—line 1996 out of 3900. Shakespeare probably wasn't counting lines, but it's not crazy to suggest he displayed here a rather consumate facility for poetic and dramatic structure.

Even after *Gonzago*, Hamlet doesn't know if Claudius knows he knows, because he still doesn't know for sure if there's anything *to* know. This is to phrase the situation in an admittedly Byzantine manner, but it aptly evokes the Italianate cat-and-mouse game that's at play. It's Hamlet's own fault, of course, that the mousetrap is a failure. Just as he loses his cool with Ophelia in the nunnery scene, undercutting his own deception (see Chapter Three), here in his manic, jibing, ad-libbed chorusing about the nephew, he frames the play wrong, presumably in order to threaten Claudius and get his goat. As a result he proves nothing, and learns nothing. He blows it.

Claudius' prayer scene after the mousetrap 3.3.36 emphasizes to the audience that the murder did occur, and that Claudius is guilty. But we already know that (those of us who weren't in conversation during his previous re pentance speech).

As Kill a King

The only other character to receive even a hint of the murder is Gertrude. It's often assumed that Hamlet reveals it to her in her closet, but a look at the conversation shows it to be oddly otherwise. Hamlet has just stabbed Polonius, but he hasn't lifted the arras yet; he still thinks it's the king who lies behind:

> Gertrude: O, what a rash and bloody deed is this!

> Hamlet: A bloody deed! almost as bad, good mother,
> As kill a king, and marry with his brother.

> Gertrude: As kill a king!

> Hamlet: Ay, lady, it was my word.

These are wild and whirling words. Hamlet is apparently accusing Gertrude of the murder. Gertrude gets an intimation that King Hamlet might have been killed, but no hint that Claudius did it. And they never return to the subject.

Eighty lines later, the ghost appears to Hamlet, but not to Gertrude, undermining any credibility that Hamlet's talk of "killing" may have had. This is odd behavior for the ghost, which we could explain by imputing various ghostly motivations. But its failure to appear to Gertrude certainly serves to continue the central dramatic device driving the action of the play—everyone's ignorance of/uncertainty about the murder. Hamlet goes to some lengths to convince Gertrude he's not crazy, but given his behavior and his misdirected and only passing reference to the killing, there's no way we can say that she "knows" of the murder.

And that is the last piece of even tenuous knowledge gained about the murder, by any character in the play. Hamlet refers to it again in conversation with Horatio ("He that hath kill'd my king" 5.2.64), but he'd already told Horatio about it. Even when Laertes reveals Claudius' perfidy—"the king's to blame"—he's not talking about King Hamlet's murder; he has no inkling of it. He's talking about the poisoned cup and blade.

So at the end, where does that leave Horatio, the only character left who has any idea that King Hamlet was murdered? He has to convince the courtiers that there was a ghost (he has the guards' word to support that, at least), that the ghost described the murder (he only heard of this from Hamlet, so the courtiers will hear it third-hand), and that it was an honest ghost (Horatio's got to wonder, so what will the courtiers think?). And he has no idea what passed between Laertes and Claudius, so he'll be hard-pressed to explain the final carnage.

Horatio may try to report Hamlet and his cause aright, but in the end, nobody will really know what happened. Excusing the meter, we could adapt Hamlet's words for Horatio: "O, cursed sprite, that ever I was born to report aright."

Where's Your Father?

That bleak prospect—of eternal uncertainty, and purposes permanently mistook—is an apt coda to the play's opening line, and a meet summation of its forever vague, doubtful, and ambiguous portrayal of knowledge.

That uncertainty of knowledge is perhaps best exemplified by the uncertain and confused textual situation for *Hamlet* itself—the multiple, partially overlapping, contradictory texts, and the many equally valid readings that are perhaps best epitomized in Hamlet's small and consumate speech on readiness and the fall of a sparrow. It's amusing to think that the author intended all that textual confusion.

Nietzsche's assertion of Hamlet's problem—that he has achieved "true knowledge," that he has "looked truly into the essence of things," and that his knowledge "inhibits action...outweighs any motive for action,"—is wrong by a hundred and eighty degrees. (He's a better philosopher than critic.) True, "action requires the veil of illusion"—why should Hamlet live or "act" when he's just going to die, and the rest is silence? But Hamlet's true achievement lies in his ability to adopt that illusion not in the face of "true knowledge," but in despite of knowing that he can never truly know.

Or perhaps that is *Hamlet*'s unique achievement, not Hamlet's.

An interesting note on this subject: The words "believe" and "belief" occur twice as frequently in *Hamlet* as in the rest of Shakespeare's works—only *Measure for Measure* exceeds it—and more than half of those usages are coupled with negatives ("believe none of us") or qualifiers ("do in part believe it").

When Honor's at the Stake

So the characters' ignorance repeatedly highlights the play's particularly modern, even existential, picture of uncertain knowledge. But Hamlet's sole knowledge is also significant because it creates such complex internal conflicts. *Hamlet* is perhaps the most internal of plays, and conflicts are, after all, the very stuff of drama.

Hamlet is constrained by three codes of honor, and they conflict, both within themselves and with each other. In his father's code—the code of Saxo's Hourendil—revenge is required. That is the single-minded code that the ghost seeks to impose on Hamlet with his repeated demands from the cellarage that he "Swear!" to revenge his father's murder.

But that code also demands, as the absolutely core value, allegiance and loyalty to the sovereign lord. So Hamlet's murder of Claudius would be a crime of the foulest nature. And since no one knows of Claudius' deed, Hamlet's revenge would be viewed as a pure play for power—a fallback to the internecine battles of earlier days that constituted "honor" for his father, and that Shakespeare depicted and vilified so unremittingly in his plays on the Wars of the Roses.

But Hamlet is also a child of the Elizabethan age. Two major shifts had occurred since Hourendil's time—to the rule of law, and to the code of Christian ethics. Revenge and personal battles, while retaining some aura of honor and glory, were directly contrary to the Christian morality that is invoked so resoundingly in the "To be or not to be" soliloquy and throughout the play. The key passage, of course, is from Romans 12:19: "Vengeance is mine; I will repay, saith the Lord."

And on the secular side, in Shakespeare's day those kinds of combative actions were just plain illegal, punishable by imprisonment or death. Will's cohort and competitor Ben Jonson went to jail and barely avoided execution for his fatal duel with Gabriel Spencer. (He had a T branded on his thumb by the ecclesiastical courts.) Christopher Marlowe went to Newgate Prison with fellow playwright Thomas Watson (another university wit) for a street fight that ended in the death of an innkeeper's son, and he was brought to law three years later for a fight in Canterbury. Under the rule of law, the ghost's word—take it as Hamlet will "for a thousand pound" 3.2.218—carries no weight.

When the ghost first makes his revelation, Hamlet (in word, at least) tosses aside all that new learning, and the new codes and commandments, for the single-minded code of revenge: 1.5.106

Yea, from the table of my memory

> I'll wipe away all trivial fond records,
> All saws of books, all forms, all pressures past
> That youth and observation copied there,
> And thy commandement all alone shall live
> Within the book and volume of my brain

Laertes does likewise in his words to Claudius: "To hell, allegiance! vows, to the blackest devil!/Conscience and grace, to the profoundest pit!/I dare damnation." 4.5.111 He yearns "To cut [Hamlet's] throat i' th' church." 4.7.126

But Hamlet can't so easily abandon the code of honor in which he was raised and educated. If he did, he'd be nothing more than a stock revenge figure—like Laertes, or the protagonist of the *Ur-Hamlet*, which was ridiculed repeatedly between 1589 and 1601 (*viz*, the line from Thomas Lodge's 1596 *Wit's Miserie and the World's Madness:* "the ghost which cried so miserably at the Theatre, like an oyster-wife, 'Hamlet, revenge.'").

Even in the final scene, Hamlet is arguing with himself (out loud to Horatio, so we can hear it) over whether it's honorable to take his revenge: "is't not perfect conscience/To quit him with this arm? And is't not to be damned,/To let this canker of our nature come/In further evil?" 5.2.76 Horatio is typically circumspect in his non-reply.

So whether you're talking about the old code, which requires allegiance to the ruler, or the new code, which requires allegiance to the law and Christian morality, the reason for Hamlet's delay is plain and simple: nobody else except Hamlet and Horatio even knows that the murder has occurred, and even Hamlet's knowledge is far from certain.

When Laertes names Claudius' villainy in his dying breath—"the King, the King's to blame." 5.2.260—on that instant, Hamlet takes his revenge. And even then, absent proof, the courtiers cry treason. It's left to Horatio to absolve him by the code of law—to, in Hamlet's words, "Report me and my cause aright/To the unsatisfied," 5.2.280 or in Horatio's words, to "speak to th' yet unknowing world." 5.2.328 And it's also left to Horatio to absolve him by the Christian code: "Good night, sweet prince,/And flights of angels sing thee to thy rest!" 5.2.305 Fortinbras, for his part, gives honor to Hamlet's actions from the world of Hourendil and King Hamlet: "The soldiers' music and the rite of war/Speak loudly for him." 5.2.350

Hamlet's final ability to act honorably within these conflicting codes, and even despite the uncertainty that permeates the play, bespeaks not only his maturation from a child to a man, but the emergence of the modern world view that so many have seen embodied in *Hamlet*. Therein lies much of the power that it carries through the generations. The play is, both for Hamlet and for us, a coming of age.

A Tragicall Hystorie of Hamlet's Age

As I said in Chapter One, I'm not the first one to be kept awake nights by the gravedigger's contradictory statements, and by their absence in Q1. At least a dozen critics over the last century and a half have come to grips with the problem. You'll find much of the nineteenth-century discussion on prince-hamlet.com, and I summarize the twentieth-century discussion at the end of this appendix.

To begin with, though, I'd like to condense the arguments to their very crux: the gravedigger's lines. All the commentators agree that there's a contradiction between those lines and the impression of Hamlet's youth given throughout the play. The question this raises: why are those lines there? And that raises a related question that needs answering in concert—when did those lines get there?

To address this, I need to give a brief explanation of current thinking on the development of the Hamlet text. (A good discussion of this is by Gary Taylor and Stanley Wells in their *William Shakespeare: A Textual Companion*.) Here's how most scholars see it these days:

1589 or before. An early version of the play (which scholars call the *Ur-Hamlet*) was written by Kyd, Shakespeare, both, and/or other(s). It may have been revised during the 1590s, in particular in 1594, when we know Shakespeare's company presented the play.

1600/1601. Shakespeare rewrote the play into substantially the form we know it. There may have been more than one rewrite in this period. It may have been on the boards by 1600, and there was at least a revision in the fall of 1601.

Between May and December, 1603. A pirated version of the play (Q1) was published. It was probably acquired through memorial reconstruction by an actor, but perhaps also with reference to some or all of an early manuscript or shorthand transcription.

1604. Shakespeare's manuscript, either his 1601 marked-up "foul copy" or a fair copy he created later—in either case, probably with some post-1601 revisions—was used to print a "good" edition (Q2). The compositor probably referred to Q1 as well, especially for the first five scenes.

1623. A transcript of Shakespeare's pre-Q1 and pre-Q2 manuscript (perhaps from the playhouse, and probably with post-1601 revisions) was used to print F1, probably with some reference to Q2 and/or its derivatives (Q3 of 1611 and Q4 of 1622).

What nobody knows with any clarity is what revisions were made to *Hamlet* at what times—by Shakespeare, other playwrights, the players, the "prompt-book" holder (if such a person existed), or by Heminges, Condell, and/or others in preparing the texts for the printing of F1.

To return to the gravedigger's lines: some critics (mainly Østerberg and Jenkins) think they have no real import regarding Hamlet's age. I find this irrelevance theory unsatisfactory given the lines' obtrusiveness, and the pervasive and coherent use of dates and durations detailed in Chapters One and Two. And most other critics agree—those lines for some reason set Hamlet's age at thirty.

So that leaves two possibilities which we need to plumb in order to discern why those lines are there.

Scenario 1: The lines were in the 1601 manuscript from the beginning. The Q1 reporter just muffed them. One explanation (Furnivall) is that Shakespeare was writing along in 1601 with this young prince in mind, and he discovered that his hero had become much more mature. So in the last act he decided to make him thirty. Or (Blackstone) he forgot what he'd done in the first four acts. Both of these explanations are, to my mind, ridiculous.

Scenario 2: The reporter got it right. The thirty-year lines were not there in 1601/02, but were revised/added between 1602 and 1604—after Q1 was stolen, and after the F1-source manuscript was created, but before the creation and publication of Q2. The lines were then added back to the pre-Q2 manuscript before the preparation of F1.

Perhaps the teenage Hamlet suggested too directly some person of power—the likes of a Rutland, Southampton, Pembroke, or Essex—and Shakespeare, ever sensitive to the political winds, wanted to take off that edge, or provide an explanatory out if challenged. Maybe something about a young Hamlet struck wrong with the new (May, 1603) King James and/or his queen, Anne of Denmark, or Shakespeare thought it might, so he did a rewrite for a performance at court. (It's been suggested that the "little eyases" passage on the War of the Theaters was removed because Anne had taken over patronage of Paul's Boys, who are being referred to there.)

Shakespeare might, for similar reason, have removed prior to Q2 the too-precise ridicule of an unnamed stage clown who keeps repeating the same jokes Q1: 1886, a passage that only appears in Q1. This would especially make sense if it was referring to William Kempe, who had left the Chamberlain's Men in 1598 or 1599, and might have rejoined briefly in late 1601/early 1602. (I'm pleased to see that I'm preceded in this conjecture by E. K. Chambers, in his 1917 edition's introduction to the play.)

Or perhaps the reverse—he found the opportunity to add allusions to some current person or event, and wove those allusions in with the grave-digger's lines. Or maybe he found opportunity to suggest that Hamlet is illegitimate, born before Gertrude and Hamlet's marriage—a suggestion argued by Steve Sohmer.

Whatever the reason, in this scenario you need only assume there was some reason for revisions after the first playings of *Hamlet*, so the revisions were made. The other scenarios require you to assume that: 1. Shakespeare included blatantly obtrusive date references that had no meaning, or 2. he forgot what he'd already written when he was writing Act Five, or 3. he changed his mind when he got to Act Five, and never went back to revise the earlier acts.

None of these seems plausible, so I choose to believe that in the 1601 manuscript Hamlet was unequivocally a youth; the gravedigger's lines were added after the reporting of Q1, but before the preparation of Q2. Edward Hubler points out in the notes to his 1987 Signet edition (p. 177) that Shakespeare would have had time for such emendations when the theaters were closed due to plague between March, 1603 and April, 1604. Aspects of Q2 were then rolled back into the pre-Q2 version for the preparation of F1.

Why were the changes made? It's anyone's guess. Based on all the connections to Shakespeare's life in the play, and based on the clear evidence for multiple revisions, I venture to suggest that *Hamlet* was something of a "lifework" for Shakespeare up to 1604, perhaps beginning as early as the 1580s. In my view, it makes most sense to believe that he returned to the work many times, perhaps even conflating multiple parallel versions at one time or another.

Some textual editors will blanch at this suggestion—they have, in fact, while others embrace the idea—as it makes it impossible to define an "authoritative" text. Be that as it may.

The Critics Speak

With the problem of the gravedigger's lines at least described, if not solved, I'd like to give a brief review here of what critics have said about Hamlet's age over the years. This is not an exhaustive review (I keep turning up more), but it does cover all of the majors and most of the minors.

There was a flurry of discussion, in particular, between 1865 and 1877, when Horace Howard Furness published his *Variorum* edition of *Hamlet*. In that edition Furness summarizes, quotes, and comments upon his predecessors in extensive footnotes that far outweigh the text of the play itself.

In his usual comprehensive fashion, Furness provides a four-page footnote on Hamlet's age (p. 391), affixed to the gravedigger's "thirty years" line. I won't repeat his summary here; you can find the whole footnote plus some of the commentaries referred to therein transcribed at princehamlet.com. I will say here, though, that while those mid-nineteenth-century commentators offered some brilliant insights, they didn't address many of the issues covered in Chapter One.

The discussion faded after the *Variorum Hamlet* was published—probably quelled by Furness's comprehensive summary. It emerged again at the beginning of the twentieth century, but with a curiously dismissive air.

A. C. Bradley devotes three pages (pp. 407–409) to Hamlet's age in a note to his 1903 *Shakespearean Tragedy* (with no firm conclusion emerging), but in the body of the book (p. 118), he abdicates with, "It matters little here whether Hamlet's age was twenty or thirty: in either case his mother was a matron of mature years." It apparently doesn't matter anywhere else, either, as in his only other mention (p. 73), he casts it aside: "the moment Burbage entered it must have been clear whether the hero was twenty or thirty."

But it matters a lot—especially when you start thinking of Gertrude as a young woman of childbearing age. (See Chapter Three.)

The redoubtable V. Østerberg published a lengthy article entitled "Prince Hamlet's Age" in 1924. Østerberg agrees that Hamlet must be a youth, but he supports his position mainly by discounting the evidence that makes him thirty. The four items in the play that explicitly cast Hamlet as an adult, in Østerberg's view, are simply setspeech-speak, dramatic license, and sloppy carelessness on Shakespeare's part, and are not intended to set Hamlet's age. They're inconsistencies, like other inconsistencies in the play, which have no import. He disdains the idea of a rewrite for Burbage. His is a cavalier approach, given the insistence and coherence of those four items, and the other date and time references throughout the play.

John Dover Wilson takes a stab at the age issue in a note on the gravedigger's thirty-year line his 1934 New Cambridge edition of the play: "This together with the insistence upon 'thirty' years of married life for the Player King and Queen and the precise reference to 'three and twenty years' since Yorick's death, fixes the age of Ham. in so pointed a fashion that as most agree Sh. clearly attached importance to it; and yet this age does not at all tally with the impression of youth and inexperience which Ham. gives us at the opening of the play. The discrepancy, prob. due to revision, has occasioned much discussion." He references Furness, Østerberg, and his own introduction, in which he says, "The most famous of [the problems], the puzzle of Hamlet's age, which seems to be about eighteen at the opening of the play and is inferentially fixed at thirty by the words of the sexton in the last act, looks like a consequence of revisions, but has obviously nothing to do with any difficulty in the original play and passes entirely unnoticed by spectators in the theatre, seeing that their Hamlet is an actor made up to represent a certain age, which they accept without question."

Then in his 1935 *What Happens in Hamlet*, Wilson ducks with the following. "There are far more pertinent questions than whether Hamlet was eighteen or thirty years of age, over which the commentators have wrangled. For while the problem of Hamlet's age is probably a textual one, and in any event poses no theatrical importance, since Hamlet is the age his impersonator makes him, that of the constitution of the state of Denmark is vital to our conception of the drama as a whole."

In a footnote to his 1936 *Preface* to *Hamlet*, Harley Granville-Barker asks about the gravedigger's lines, "Why does Shakespeare take the trouble, thus late in the day, to establish Hamlet's age so exactly?" He suggests that Shakespeare created the discrepancy intentionally, for literary and dramatic effect: "To counteract the impression the youthful prince...will have made on us; and thus late in the day, because, with the great central mass of the play's thought and passion behind him, Hamlet is inevitably a maturer figure than was the morbid young rebel of its beginning."

Harold Jenkins, whose comments I referred to in Chapter One, follows Østerberg's lead in a long note to his 1982 Arden edition of the play (p. 551). He discounts the significance of the thirty-year statements, stating that they are formulaic usages familiar in dramatic tradition, "introduced not because of but in spite of what they imply about Hamlet's age." Unlike Østerberg, he comes to no conclusion on Hamlet's age.

To reiterate what I've already said in Chapter One, Professor Bloom's discussion of Hamlet's age in his 1998 *Shakespeare: The Invention of the Human* ("none of this matters: he is always both the youngest and the oldest person ality in the drama") is less than satisfying.

There are some good arguments and good writing among all this commentary. Jenkins, in particular, is quite cogent, as is Minto in his 1875 discussions. I encourage you to read them at princehamlet.com, and form your own opinion.

Hamlet, Parnassus, and the War of the Theaters

If you've read the rest of this book, you've no doubt noticed my fascination for Shakespeare's relationship to St. John's College, Cambridge, and its history of dramatic presentations—in particular the three *Parnassus* plays put on by St. John's students at their Christmas revels in the three years 1599/1600 to 1601/02. These plays' references to Shakespeare and to the Elizabethan "poet's war" between rival playwrights and acting companies (the *poetomachia*, as Thomas Dekker, one of its participants, styled it) form a fascinating little web of allusions relating to *Hamlet* that I haven't seen fully explored elsewhere.

First, to encapsulate Will's connections to St. John's:

- His patron, Henry Wriothesley, Earl of Southampton, attended St. John's from 1586 to 1589.

- Southampton's guardian, Lord Burghley (who many think is figured to some extent in Polonius—see Appendix C), attended St. John's in the late 1530s and early 1540s. His son Robert Cecil (possibly figured in Laertes) attended from 1579.

- Edward de Vere, Earl of Oxford (another of Burghley's wards), who was a playwright and had his own company, and who is arguably heavily alluded to in *Hamlet* (again, see Appendix C), graduated from St. John's in 1564.

- John Dee, who advised Elizabeth and Burghley on the 1582 papal calendar revision (see Appendix D) and who hosted the Chamberlain's Men at his home in Mortlake in 1603, took his B. A. from St. John's in 1545.

- The two *Return to Parnassus* plays, put on at St. John's in 1600/01 and 1601/02, both refer to Shakespeare directly. As discussed here, the first play also foreshadows *Hamlet*.

- The playwright and pamphleteer Thomas Nashe, who pilloried the *Ur-Hamlet* creator in 1589 (see Chapter Four), graduated Master of Arts from St. John's in 1586. The antihero of the *Return to Parnassus* plays is a thinly disguised rendition of Nashe (also discussed in Chapter Four).

- Robert Greene, Nashe's compatriot, another of Shakespeare's attackers discussed in Chapter Four, and author of *Alphonsus* (see below), attended St. John's from 1575 to 1578.

- Per the title page of the First Quarto, *Hamlet* was played by Shakespeare's company at the university of Cambridge. Given its long-standing theatrical tradition (along with its neighbor, Trinity), St. John's Hall was a likely venue for those performances.

- The accounts of the revels season at St. John's in 1607/08 have an uncanny chronological relation to the dates in *Hamlet* (discussed in more detail in Chapter Two).

These connections don't add up to an intimate relationship, but combined with the insights below, they do suggest a strong mutual awareness between Will and the theatrical element at St. John's, notably the anonymous St. John's student(s) who penned *Return Parts I* and *II*.

A Clown's Head

There's one connection in *Return, Part I* that I haven't seen discussed elsewhere. One of the protagonists, Philomusus, has been forced to take a job as a country sexton, digging graves. He's bemoaning his lot to his compatriot Studioso, but tries to make light of it (Leishman edition: l. 667):

"Yet the best is I meet now and then with a clown's head, that is as good to one as the poesie, *ut hora sic vita* [as an hour, so is life], ready to put me in mind of the end of this my misery."

It's remarkably reminiscent of the gravedigger scene.

This play was performed at Christmas, 1600/01—less than a year before Shakespeare's final *Hamlet* debuted. Given all of Will's connections to St. John's, I can't help but wonder whether he saw that performance or read a script, and found there a seed for Yorick and the gravedigger. And given the obsession with time and haste in *Hamlet,* might not *Parnassus*'s "hora" also have been one inspiration for the name of Hamlet's closest compatriot—Horatio, or "hour man"?

Giving the Poets a Pill

The other connection, which I discuss in another context in Chapter Four, is in *Return, Part II.* Burbage and Kemp are getting ready to audition the itinerant scholars Philomusus and Studioso, and Kemp comments on university playwrights:

Few of the university men pen plays well, they smell too much of that writer Ovid, and that writer Metamorphosis, and talk too much of Proserpina and Jupiter. Why here's our fellow Shakespeare puts them all down, ay and Ben Jonson too. And that Ben Jonson is a pestilent fellow, he brought up Horace giving the Poets a pill, but our fellow Shakespeare hath given him a purge that made him beray his credit.

The "pill" refers to a scene in Jonson's *Poetaster,* part of the War of the Theaters—a battle of parody, invective, and satire waged between playwrights Ben Jonson, John Marston, and Thomas Dekker (with help from others) between 1598 and 1601. The battles were waged through plays performed by the Chamberlain's Men and by the boys' companies—the Children of Paul's (set up in 1599) and Children of the Chapel (1600). These boys' companies had a complex relationship to the Chamberlain's Men, both competitive and cooperative.

I won't attempt to detail the whole war here; as in real wars, there were all sorts of side-skirmishes and confused alarms. There's a lengthy discussion in *The Cambridge History of English and American Literature* on Bartelby.com.

For discussing the War's relation to *Hamlet,* though, it's handy to have a simple chronological cheat sheet, something I haven't found elsewhere. (This is based mainly on E. K. Chambers' 1951 *Elizabethan Stage*, which is more authoritative than the 1907–1921 *Cambridge History*. There are disagreements regarding authorship and dates; this abbreviated list is hence inaccurate due to its necessary omissions.) I've included *Hamlet*, the *Parnassus* plays, and a couple of others in the chronology, for reasons that will become obvious.

Autumn 1599	The anonymous (mostly by Marston) *Histriomastix* parodies Jonson and public players.	Paul's Boys
Winter 1599/1600	Jonson replies with *Every Man Out of his Humour.*	Chamberlains' Men
1600	The anonymous (Marston again) *Jack Drum's Entertainment* casts Jonson as a cuckold.	Paul's Boys
1600	Jonson's *Cynthia's Revels* satirizes Marston and Dekker.	Children of the Chapel
Christmas 1600/01	*Return to Parnassus, Part I*. Refers to Shakespeare, and perhaps foreshadows *Hamlet*.	St. John's
Spring 1601	Jonson's *Poetaster* (proleptically responding to news of the imminent *Satiromastix* and/or *What You Will*) satirizes Marston and Dekker.	Children of the Chapel
Summer/fall 1601	Decker's *Satiromastix* (with Marston?) responds to *Cynthia's Revels* and *Poetaster*.	Paul's Boys and Chamberlain's Men
Summer/fall 1601	Marston parodies Jonson in *What You Will* (written before *Poetaster*, but revised afterward, then performed).	Paul's Boys
July, 1601	Dekker and Munday's *Jephthah*	Admiral's Men
August, 1601	Greene's *Alphonsus King of Arragon*	Admiral's Men
Fall 1601	*Hamlet* written/rewritten and debuted.	Chamberlain's Men
December 1601	*Return to Parnassus, Part II* written	St. John's

	(probably played at New Year's). Refers to *Poetaster,* and to Shake-speare's "purge" in reply.	

The battle may have started out in earnest, but it apparently continued at least in part because it sold seats (as Rosencrantz suggests in the passage cited below). By 1603 all the playwrights involved were working together, and in 1604 Marston dedicated his *Malcontent* to Jonson in quite gracious terms.

In the scene from Jonson's *Poetaster* referred to in *Parnassus* ("he brought up Horace giving the Poets a pill"), Horace (Jonson) gives Crispinus (Marston) a pill that causes him to vomit up a whole lexicon of affected language. Scholars have gone through incredible contortions to explain what "purge" Shakespeare administered to Jonson. In my opinion, none of the explanations has been even reasonably satisfying. But perhaps the answer is obvious, residing in the *Hamlet* passage on the War of the Theaters which is so familiar (and which only appears in full in F1). For your convenience, I'll quote it here in full. 2.2.254

Hamlet: …What players are they?

Rosencrantz: Even those you were wont to take such delight in, the tragedians of the city.

Hamlet: How chances it they travel? Their residence, both in reputation and profit, was better both ways.

Rosencrantz: I think their inhibition comes by the means of the late innovation.

Hamlet: Do they hold the same estimation they did when I was in the city? Are they so follow'd?

Rosencrantz: No indeed are they not.

[F1 only:
Hamlet: How comes it? do they grow rusty?

Rosencrantz: Nay, their endeavor keeps in the wonted pace; but there is, sir, an aery of children, little eyases, that cry out on the top of question, and are most tyrannically clapp'd for't. These are now the fashion, and so berattle the common stages—so they call them—that many wearing rapiers are afraid of goose-quills and dare scarce come thither.

Hamlet: What, are they children? Who maintains 'em? How are they escoted? Will they pursue the quality no longer than they can sing? Will they not say afterwards, if they should grow themselves to common players (as it is most like, if their means are no better), their writers do them wrong, to make them exclaim against their own succession?

Rosencrantz: Faith, there has been much to do on both sides, and the nation holds it no sin to tarre them to controversy. There was for a while no money bid for argument, unless the poet and the player went to cuffs in the question.

Hamlet: Is't possible?

Guildenstern: O, there has been much throwing about of brains.

Hamlet: Do the boys carry it away?

Rosencrantz: Ay, that they do, my lord—Hercules and his load too.]

Rosencrantz suggests that the boys' companies' success has cut the public players' take at the gate to the point that they have to go on provincial tour. That success was augmented by the popularity of personal attacks by the poets on each other and on players, and by gentlemen's titillating fear of attack by those poets. (*Poetaster*, from the spring of 1601, puts across the difficulty in the preceding winter—"this winter has made us all poorer than so many starved snakes." It also imparts the gentlemen's concern about being ridiculed by the playwrights: "Your courtier cannot kiss his mistress's slipper, in quiet, for them.")

The "innovation"—which in every other Shakespearian usage is related to rebellion and unrest—may refer to various things. Some have suggested the Essex Rebellion in February 1601, and the tangential role the Chamberlain's Men played in that. Others think it refers to the rise of the boys' companies and the private theaters. Or it could be referring internally, to the threat from Fortinbras and his "resolutes." "Hercules," bearing the world on his shoulders, was on the sign outside the Globe.

The Croaking Raven Doth Bellow for Revenge

This little F1 allusion to the *poetomachia*, however, is only part of a larger pattern of references to the contemporary theater scene that runs through the play. J. D. Wilson has made a strong case—notably in Appendix C of *What Happens in Hamlet*—that the players in *Hamlet* are a takeoff on Henslowe and Alleyn's Admiral's Men, the leading public competitors to the Chamberlain's Men. I'll summarize Wilson's argument here, with a few glosses of my own.

- The players—with their bombastic Hecuba speech, old-fashioned dumb show, stagey acting, and purple poetry—are a burlesque of an outdated and overblown tragic style. [Dumb shows were often used to add some semblance of theatricality to the endless narrative verse declamation of Senecan-style tragedies.]

- Rosencrantz's description of the players as "tragedians of the city" 2.2.255 points to the Admiral's Men, whose main stock included Marlowe's tragedies and Kyd's *The Spanish Tragedy* [and I might add yet another revenge tragedy, Greene's *Orlando Furioso*], and whose leading actor, Alleyn, was famous almost solely as a tragedian.

- Hamlet's "When Roscius was an actor in Rome" 2.2.279 would immediately bring to mind Alleyn. Says Wilson (with five supporting examples), "'Roscius' was the title almost universally conferred at that time upon Alleyn."

- Hamlet's Jephthah sally against Polonius 2.2.285 echoes Dekker and Munday's *Jephthah*, which was played by the Admiral's Men in July 1601, just months before the composition and first playings of *Hamlet* as we know it.

- The Hecuba speech has some significant connection to the lost *Dido and Aeneas,* performed by the Admiral's Men on January 8, 1598. (It's possible that Jonson had a hand in this play.)

- The last sentence of Hamlet's "Begin, murtherer; leave thy damnable faces and begin. Come, the croaking raven doth bellow for revenge" 3.2.192 is a twist on a speech from the anonymous old (1591–92) *True Tragedy of Richard III* ("The screeking Raven sits croking for revenge./Whole heads of beasts come bellowing for revenge."). This play was quite possibly a property of the Admiral's Men; Henslowe advanced money to Jonson on June 27, 1602 for a play book called *Richard Crookback*, which suggests a revision of a version earlier presented. [It seems that it must have been played more recently than ten years back, for Will to have brought the quotation to mind.] [The allusion to this speech cracks at least four jokes simultaneously; see princehamlet.com.]

There's further evidence that Wilson doesn't mention but that A. C. Bradley does, in a footnote to his long note on Hamlet's age in *Shakespearean Tragedy.* Gonzago's "full thirty years" lines in the mousetrap play mimic lines from our friend Robert Greene's *Alphonsus King of Aragon.* Here are Greene's lines, which in 1601 were probably delivered by Alleyn of the Admiral's Men (Malone Society edition, line 1259):

> Thrice ten times Phoebus with his golden beams
> Hath compassed the circle of the sky,
> Thrice ten times Ceres hath her workmen hir'd,
> And fill'd her barns with fruitful crops of corn,
> Since first in priesthood I did lead my life.

This echo is not so surprising; E. K. Chambers tells us (*Elizabethan Stage,* III, 327) that the Admiral's men revived this 1587 play in August, 1601—again, just before *Hamlet*'s debut. (The Admiral's Men actually purchased the script from Alleyn.) The triggering conflict in *Alphonsus* is tellingly familiar: the usurpation of the crown of Aragon by the king's murderous younger brother. The son of the rightful heir (grandson of Alphonsus the murdered king, grandnephew of the usurper) says in Act 1: (Malone Society edition, line 139)

> Next to *Alphonsus* should my father [Carinus] come,

For to possesse the Diadem by right
Of *Aragon,* but that the wicked wretch,
His [Alphonsus's] yonger brother, with aspiring mind,
By secret treason robd him [Alphonsus] of his life,
And me his [Carinus's] sonne, of that which was my due.

If you combine Rosencrantz and Hamlet's discussion of the War of the Theaters with Wilson's demonstration that the whole players section is among other things an extended takeoff on the Admiral's Men and Jonson, you can see in *Hamlet* a final and conclusive sally in that war. "Gentle," "sweet" Shakespeare brings the acrimonious battle to a close. Pretty much everybody gets ridiculed in his final skirmish, including his own young hero.

Given the timing of all this, isn't it most likely that *Hamlet* is itself the "purge" that *Parnassus* refers to? *Poetaster* is played in the spring, *Satiro-mastix* and *What You Will* are played in the summer and fall, *Hamlet* con cludes the battle—swatting good-humoredly at Will's friend and colleague Jonson—in October/November, and the *Parnassus* playwright comments on the whole imbroglio in December. I find that E. K. Chambers came to a similar surmise in his 1917 edition of *Hamlet* (though only in a passing mention), and he even goes so far as to suggest, based on the *Parnassus* references, that *Hamlet* was played at Cambridge in October, 1601 or thereabouts.

There's even a reference in *Hamlet* to a purge, and in telling proximity to the whole players business. Just after the mousetrap, Guildenstern assaults Hamlet regarding Claudius: 3.2.229

Guildenstern: The King, sir—

Hamlet: Ay, sir, what of him?

Guildenstern: Is in his retirement marvellous distemp'red.

Hamlet: With drink, sir?

Guildenstern: No, my lord, with choler.

Hamlet: Your wisdom should show itself more richer to signify this
to the doctor, for for me to put him to his purgation would perhaps
plunge him into more choler.

Choler was one of the four "humours," which were the central conceits of
Jonson's plays *Every Man in His Humour* (1598) and the poetomachian
Every Man Out of His Humour (1599). The conflation of humours with pur-
gation once again rings of Jonson and the War of the Theaters.

This web of allusions is nothing certain; absent some remarkable discovery, no explanation promises to be. But viewing *Hamlet* as *Parnassus'* purge
is a simple, coherent, and satisfying solution to that vexing question. (And it
explains some great jokes.) It adds one more set of threads to the tapestry,
both inside and outside the play, that has delighted audiences, scholars, and
readers for four hundred years.

Thirty Dozen Moons: How Many Years Had Gertrude the Queen?

As I was sorting through the four key pieces of evidence that seem to set Hamlet's age at thirty (see Chapter One), I kept running up against the Player King's opening lines from the Gonzago play: 3.2.102

> Full thirty times hath Phœbus' cart [the sun] gone round
> Neptune's salt wash and Tellus' orbed ground,
> And thirty dozen moons with borrow'd sheen
> About the world have times twelve thirties been,
> Since love our hearts and Hymen did our hands
> Unite commutual in most sacred bands.

It seems that this kind of insistent dating must mean something, especially in relation to the gravedigger's thirty-year statements. Like Hamlet's "galls his kibe" line in the graveyard, this has always smacked to me of a topical allusion.

Steve Sohmer tackled this passage in detail in his "Certain Speculations on Hamlet, the Calendar, and Martin Luther," asserting that it demonstrates

Hamlet's illegitimacy (an item I won't address here). He calculates the timing as follows. For discussion of the "synodic" months that Sohmer uses versus "sidereal" months, see the calendar-related links at princehamlet.com. Suffice it here to say that using synodic months makes the most sense.

360 synodic months at 29.53 days per month = 10,631 days
Add 30 days, for 10,661 days total

I propose in Chapter Two that the mousetrap was played on January 5, 1602, and that the murder figured in the mousetrap occurred on September 6, 1601. The Gonzago speech, if it has any topical date significance, is figuring back from one of those dates. Figuring back using Professor Sohmer's 10,661 days, you come up with the following:

Event	Date	Date minus 10,661 days
Murder	Sept. 6, 1601	June 29, 1572
Mousetrap	January 5, 1602	Oct. 28, 1572

The Marriage of Frederick II of Denmark

I then went looking for events that might align with those dates, and came upon a likely candidate: Frederick II, king of Denmark and Norway, was married on July 20, 1572. Since the Gonzago speech is referring to the marriage of a Danish king and queen (though the players don't know that), the reference back to Frederick's marriage seems a likely allusion for Shakespeare to have woven into his web.

There are several interesting connections that give some support. It was Frederick who hosted Shakespeare's (future?) colleagues Kemp, Bryan, and Pope in 1586 at Elsinore. Frederick's daughter was Anne, who in 1589 married James VI of Scotland—the future (1603) James I of Great Britain. When Shakespeare was writing Hamlet in late 1601, court circles were well aware of Elizabeth's infirmity and James' likely accession, and many were maneuvering for favor with the possible successor. Shakespeare was remarkably sensitive to the nuances of court politics (more so than many of his competitors, who were forever getting censored or thrown in the dock for violating political sensitivities), so a nod to the future queen—a lover and patron of theater—would not be surprising.

But the date doesn't line up exactly—it's three weeks off. If Shakespeare was calculating his dates so carefully, it doesn't seem likely he would have made this error. And while there are some persuasive articles demonstrating Shakespeare's knowledge of astronomical details (see Appendix D), it just seems unlikely that he went so far as to calculate synodic months to the second decimal.

Even if he calculated to one decimal point (29.5 days per month), he'd be off by ten days (July 10, not July 20). That discrepancy could be explained by the 10-day difference between the Julian calendar then in use in England versus the Gregorian calendar adopted in 1582 by Catholic countries, but Denmark was also on the Julian calendar at the time; it all feels like a serious stretch.

The Oxford/Cecil Connection

A more likely prospect came from an unlikely source—that schismatic sect of Shakespeare-authorship contrarians who claim that Edward de Vere, Earl of Oxford, actually wrote the Shakespeare plays. Tom Bethell gives the most cogent summary that I've seen, in his 1991 *Atlantic Monthly* article "The Case for Oxford." In Bethell's words:

- Lord Burghley wrote out a set of precepts ("Towards thy superiors be humble yet generous; with thine equals familiar yet respective") strongly reminiscent of the advice Polonius gives to Laertes ("Be thou familiar but by no means vulgar...."). Burghley's precepts, intended for the use of his son Robert, were published in 1618. *Hamlet* first appeared in quarto in 1603. Edmund K. Chambers, one of the leading Shakespeare scholars of the twentieth century, offered the following explanation: "Conceivably Shakespeare knew a pocket manuscript."

- In Act II Polonius sends Reynaldo to spy on Laertes in Paris, possibly catching him "drinking, fencing, swearing, quarreling," or "falling out at tennis." In real life Burghley's older son, Thomas Cecil, did go to Paris, whence the well-informed Burghley somehow received information, through a secret channel, of Thomas's "inordinate love of...dice and cards." Oxford, incidentally, did have a real and widely noted "falling out at tennis"—not a widely practiced sport in those days—with Sir Philip Sidney, the Earl of Leicester's nephew.

- Oxford and Hamlet are similar figures, courtiers and Renaissance men of varied accomplishments; both were scholars, athletes, and poets. Many critics have noted Hamlet's resemblance to Castiglione's beau ideal in *The Courtier*. At the age of twenty-one, Oxford wrote a Latin introduction to a translation of this book. Both Oxford and Hamlet were patrons of play-acting companies.

- In 1573 Oxford contributed a preface to an English translation of *Cardanas Comfort*, a book of consoling advice which the orthodox scholar Hardin Craig called "Hamlet's book." The book includes passages from which Hamlet's soliloquy was surely taken ("What should we account of death to be resembled to anything better than sleep....We are assured not only to sleep, but also to die....").

- Oxford stabbed a servant of Burghley's (possibly another of Burghley's spies). Polonius is stabbed by Hamlet while spying on him.

- Hamlet's trusted friend is Horatio. Oxford's most trusted relative seems to have been Horace Vere, called Horatio in some documents (and so named by the *Dictionary of National Biography*).

- Oxford, like Hamlet, was captured by pirates en route to England; both participated in sea battles.

Put aside the loony idea that Oxford wrote Shakespeare's plays; it's far more likely that Shakespeare was aware of these Oxford-related items—that they exerted an influence (consciously or unconsciously) when he was writing. My characterization in Chapter Four of Hamlet as a somewhat pettish aristocrat adds further to these seeming connections; Oxford was not a pleasant character. I note also that Oxford was a 1564 graduate of St. John's College, Cambridge, which connection to Shakespeare I discuss at some length in Appendix B. While this is all interesting, I really became intrigued when I discovered that Oxford married Burghley's daughter Anne in December, 1571.

Now suppose that the Gonzago speech was taking a more mundane approach to dating, saying that the king and queen's marriage happened thirty years and one month past. If the mousetrap was played in January, 1602, you can easily count back to December, 1571. If Shakespeare did intend such an allusion, he presumably would have wanted some of his readers and auditors to get it, so this simple calculation makes more sense.

On further perusal, I discovered that in fact there were three other important marriages in that same week, December 16–23, 1571.

- Henry Somerset, Earl of Worcester, and Elizabeth Hastings, daughter of the Earl of Huntingdon.

- Edward Dudley, Earl of Sutton, and Katherine Brydges, sister of the Baron Chandos.

- Thomas, Lord Paget, married Nazaret (née Newton), widow of Sir Thomas Southwell.

E. K. Chambers thinks it possible that the queen attended all of these weddings. An allusion to this flurry of high-profile marriages—especially Oxford's—doesn't require resort to abstruse calendrical arithmetic, and it explains the player king's lines independently of Hamlet's age.

Shakespeare, the Calendar, the Catholics, and The Stars

Given the number and scope of the calendar-related correlations that I detail in Chapter Two, any reasonable person has to ask, "Did Shakespeare really pay that much attention to the calendar? Could he possibly have had all this seemingly arcane knowledge, or the interest necessary to infuse calendar references throughout the play?"

First, I refer you to the selection of online articles on the subject at princehamlet.com. If those leave any doubt, a few hours spent with E. K. Chambers' *Mediaeval Stage* (1903) and *Elizabethan Stage* (1923) should quell it. These books (six volumes in all) provide an incredibly detailed account of the emergence of drama from the church liturgy, and drama's ongoing relationship to the liturgical calendar into the sixteenth and early seventeenth centuries. Consider also Steve Sohmer's *Shakespeare's Mystery Play*, which collects revisions of his online articles plus additional material into a remarkably convincing if unfortunately somewhat motley and uneven collection; Francois Laroque's *Shakespeare's Festive World*, which discusses at length the links between Shakespeare's plays and the liturgical calendar; and

David Wiles' *Shakespeare's Almanac*, which addresses the use of the calendar in *Midsummer Night's Dream* in a manner similar to Steve Sohmer's work.

Elizabethan dramatic companies were also especially attuned to the another calendar: the "terms" of the law courts (which were based on some fairly abstruse calendar calculations). In *Elizabethan Stage* (I, 329), E. K. Chamber explains that theaters' "profits swelled in term time and dwindled in vacation." This is because the students and lawyers of Grey's Inn, the Middle Temple, and other inns of court were in town, and likewise the royal courtiers; the law terms set the term for London's social season. Those men were among the theaters' best (and most perspicacious) customers; they took the more expensive seats in the upper galleries, and also hired the companies to present plays at their inns on special occasions.

In this appendix I'd like to look at some lesser-known articles about Shakespeare and the calendar, and the obviously and not-so-obviously related subjects of astronomy, religion, and politics.

To begin with, though, I need to give a quick explanation of the calendar in Shakespeare's day. (See princehamlet.com for links to web sites on this subject.) The Julian calendar that had been used in Europe since 45 BCE was flawed; it pegged the length of a year at 365.25 days (which is off by .0075 days—ten minutes, 48 seconds). So over the centuries the calendar got out of synch with the sun. By the sixteenth century, the solstices and equinoxes had shifted by ten days. Summer solstice—the actual longest day of the year— had moved from June 21 to June 11. Christmas, likewise, was being celebrated ten days off.

This really wreaked havoc with the calculations for the lunar-based liturgical holidays—the "moveable feasts" based on the calculation of Easter. So in 1595, for instance, Easter fell on April 20, when it should have been on April 2. People *really* didn't like celebrating the Lord's birth or resurrection on the wrong day. It was a big deal.

To understand just how important it was, check out the detailed liturgical calendar that takes up more than two dozen pages at the beginning of the 1559 Book of Common Prayer. Elizabethans saw this "Kalendar" every day in church. They knew the liturgical holidays just as Americans know the date of Thanksgiving, or Jews know the date of Passover. Or consider that John Dee, Royal Astrologer, chose the date for Elizabeth's coronation. It was common practice to set important events on astrologically "propitious" days.

Legal, liturgical, and astrological calendars were touchstones for everyday life (and literature) in Elizabethan England, which explains why the popular calendar almanacs—similar to today's *Farmer's Almanac*—were among the bestselling books of the day.

Calendar Reform and the Catholic Threat

In 1582 Pope Gregory declared a new calendar to fix the Julian problem. It corrected for the ten-day error by simply eliminating them (the day after October 4 was October 15), and adjusted leap years to keep things in line for future centuries. The Catholic countries adopted the calendar immediately.

But in Protestant countries—England being a leader among those countries—politics interfered. The schism between Catholicism and Protestantism was of course the overriding European conflict of the sixteenth century. People were being burned, hanged, beheaded, and eviscerated (independently, consecutively, or simultaneously) for their beliefs throughout Mary and Elizabeth's reigns.

Elizabeth's secretary of state Burghley and spymaster Walsingham steadily maintained that they only executed people for treasonous actions, not for their faith. Many prominent but circumspect Catholic "recusants" celebrated the mass in England under Elizabeth and James. Evangelical (and especially political) Catholics, however—Jesuits in particular—were at significant risk because of the government's ever-present fear of Catholic attempts to overthrow Elizabeth and even invade England. A Catholic fifth column and Catholic "infiltration" for political reasons were real, present, and ongoing dangers.

With these currents at play, England was not eager to take up the new Catholic calendar. Not invented here.

Shakespeare and the Catholic Calendar

An eighteenth-century discovery and a lot of recent research put Shakespeare right in the thick of this Catholic/Protestant controversy. In 1757, a workman repairing the roof of Shakespeare's childhood home—the Henley Street house in Stratford—discovered a document between the tiles and the rafters that has come to be known as John Shakespeare's Spiritual Last Will and Testament. You can find good discussions of its provenance and authenticity in Stanley Wells' *A Dictionary of Shakespeare* and Anthony Holden's *William Shakespeare*.

The document is an open profession of John Shakespeare's Catholic faith, in a document of the type that were promulgated by clandestine Jesuit priests in England in the 1580s. As Park Honan points out in his 1998 Shakespeare biography, and as Richard Wilson points out in his article "Shakespeare and the Jesuits," there were many other radical Catholic influences in Will's early life, notably two of his schoolmasters at Stratford. (The schoolmaster from 1579 to 1581, John Cottam, had a brother who was a Jesuit priest and was executed at Tyburn in 1581; John left Stratford at that time, and lived as a recusant until his death.)

I'm not saying that Will was a Catholic in practice or belief. Though some claim it, there isn't enough evidence to support the contention. But it's clear that he was personally and intimately touched by the controversy from his earliest years. There's much in the plays that echoes that influence, from the obvious to the oblique.

The all-important church calendar played a key role in the controversy. An article by Robert Poole, "John Dee and the English Calendar: Science, Religion And Empire" (expanded and included in his book *Time's Altera-tion: Calendar Reform in Early Modern England*), shows how Elizabeth's government in 1582 and 1583 came to reject Gregory's papal bull instituting the new calendar. It also shows how important the decision was, involving the highest levels of power, both secular and sacred. Here's a brief *precis* of Poole's fine article:

- Frances Walsingham (Elizabeth's Secretary of State and Controller of Intelligence) received a copy of the bull in December, 1582 in diplomatic correspondence. He passed it on to John Dee [Royal Astrologer, mathematician, navigation consultant, mystic, and alchemist], asking him to evaluate it for the privy council.

- Dee replied on February 26, 1583 with a 62-page illustrated manuscript: *A playne Discourse and humble Advise for our Gratious Queen Elizabeth, her most Excellent Majestie to peruse and consider, as concerning the needful Reformation of the Vulgar Kalendar for the civile years and daies accompt-ing, or verifyeng, according to the time truly spent.* As far as I can find, no transcription of this document is available in print or electronic form. (Though you can purchase a not-terribly-legible photocopy of the original—in Elizabethan secretary hand—from the Bodleian Library by requesting MS Ashmole 1789, fos 1-62. Mine cost $39 including postage.)

- Dee's treatise recommended a variation on the Gregorian calendar (which was based on calculations back to the Council of Nicea in 325 ACE), a variation calculating back to the birth of Christ. Among other things, it recommended a shift of eleven days instead of ten. He suggested that Elizabeth proclaim this calendar to supercede the Gregorian, thereby taking the lead among the Protestant countries and co-opting the Pope. In Poole's words, "England would lead a sort of protestant counter-reformation of the calendar."

- Burghley (Lord Treasurer) agreed with Dee's treatise, but proposed a ten-day change only, hoping to convince the Catholics to drop another day in the future. He sent the treatise, with his proposed amendment, for review by some university experts: Henry Savile, John Chambers, and Thomas Digges. These experts agreed with the Dee/Burghley compromise.

- When submitted to the Bishops, the whole reform was rejected on various grounds, primarily that England could not support any Papal bull. (England finally went Gregorian in 1752.)

Did Shakespeare ever see Dee's letter? We'll probably never know—any more than we'll know if he saw the 1584 letter from Burghley to his son Robert Cecil which is perhaps mimicked in Polonius's advice to Laertes (see Appendix C). But there are some clear connections between Shakespeare and the group of scholars who were revolutionizing the calendar, and doing it based on a new astronomical view of the earth's place in the universe. These were the same people advising Pope Gregory and Queen Elizabeth on calendar reform.

Hamlet and the Infinite Universe

Peter Usher makes a strong case for Shakespeare's understanding of this astronomical revolution—and for its allegorical expression in *Hamlet*—in "Hamlet's Transformation." Again, I will briefly summarize his article, with some commentary of my own in brackets.

- While many or most people in Shakespeare's day clung to the old Ptolemaic "earth-centered" model of the universe, there was a strong and growing body of scholars who were advocating the sun-centered model espoused in the Polish astronomer Copernicus' 1543 *De revolutionibus. De revolutionibus* was published in Germany through the efforts of Georg Joachim Rheticus of the University of Wittenberg.

- John Dee championed the heliocentric model in England as early as 1556, and Thomas Digges [scientist, mathematician, member of parliament for Southampton, and one of the scholars consulted on Dee's treatise] published his own Copernican model of the universe in 1576. His big leap forward was the concept of the infinite universe, unbounded by the celestial spheres.

- Tycho Brahe—another Wittenberger—in 1588 proposed a competing hybrid model clinging to the geocentric (and finite) approach—with the planets revolving around the sun but the earth and moon remaining the center of the sun and moon's orbits. Brahe knew his English compatriots. In 1590 he sent a letter to Thomas Savile [another of the consultants on the Dee treatise] asking that he be remembered to Digges [and Dee]. He included four copies of a portrait of himself that included his family shields labeled with the names of his great-great-grandparents: Sophie Gyldenstierne and Eric Rosenkrantz. Brahe was at the time constructing his observatory, Uraniborg, near Helsingor Castle [Elsinore], which was under construction by the King of Denmark.

- Usher then argues for an allegorical representation in *Hamlet* of this competition between the finite and infinite universes—with young Hamlet representing the infinite Diggesian model, Claudius (*i.e.* Claudious Ptolemaeus) representing the old Ptolemaic system, and Rosencrantz and Guildenstern representing the intermediate (but still finite) Tychonic approach. [It's alluring to also find the Gregorian/Julian contention played out in this dissension; Sohmer makes a good case for just such an allegorical calendar contention in *Julius Caesar*.]

- Shakespeare was quite familiar with the Digges family. [The most significant connections: Digges's mother married Thomas Russell, one of two overseers of Shakespeare's will, and Digges's younger brother Leonard wrote epistles to Shakespeare for the 1623 First Folio and for the 1640 edition of his poems.]

I note that there is also at least one connection between Shakespeare and John Dee. A royal chamber accounts item for December 2, 1603—two years after *Hamlet*'s debut—records a payment of 30 pounds to "John Hymyngs one of his majesty's players…For the paynes and expences of himself and the rest of the company in coming from Mortelake in the countie of Surrie unto the courte aforesaid [at Wilton] and there p'senting before his majesty one playe." Mortlake was the site of Dee's estate; Elizabeth is recorded as having visited it multiple times.

Given the revels season and that the whole company was at Mortlake, they were most likely there for playing. This doesn't prove an acquaintance between Shakespeare and Dee, but it does suggest at least an awareness. (It's fascinating to imagine Shakespeare in Dee's library—at that time the greatest in England.) And it certainly shows, once again, the type of audience Will was writing for—not just the penny-pit audience at the Globe, but the very type of highly educated scholars and aristocrats who were leading the astronomical and calendrical revolutions of the day.

A further connection: Dee took his B. A. at St. John's College, Cambridge, in 1545, shortly after William Cecil, the future Lord Burghley. He was heavily involved in the dramatic scene while he was there. See Appendix B for Shakespeare's many connections to St. John's.

Astronomical Language in *Hamlet*

I would like to add one more discussion that supports the importance of astronomy in *Hamlet*, and the assertion that Shakespeare made special use of it. I analyzed the use of astronomy-related words in the play, and compared their frequency in fourteen other Shakespeare plays. You can see from the table below that these words are significantly more common in *Hamlet* than in the rest of the plays.

Occurrences and Frequency of Astronomy-Related Words

Word	Hamlet		Other Plays		Difference in Frequency
	Count	Frequency	Count	Frequency	
star(s)	10	.031%	40	.012%	+161%
planet(s)	1	.003%	2	.001%	+421%
firmament	1	.003%	3	.001%	+247%
sphere(s)	2	.006%	8	.002%	+161%
infinite	4	.012%	8	.002%	+421%
globe	1	.003%	5	.001%	+108%
Totals:	19	.059%	66	.020%	+200%

Overall, astronomical words occur three times as frequently in *Hamlet* as in other Shakespeare plays. It's pretty apparent that astronomy was on the playwright's mind when he was writing *Hamlet*. The theater in which he had become a part owner just a few years before, after all, was named after the most immediate of celestial objects. A globe hung as its emblem outside the front door, and the ceiling of the stage was painted with a celestial sky (to which Shakespeare alludes in more than one play). Given the multiple attestations we have of Richard Burbage's skill as a painter (he was commissioned to paint and Shakespeare to write the inscription for an "impressa," or shield, for the Earl of Rutland in 1613, for instance), it's not unreasonable to imagine that Burbage executed that painting, with the detailed astronomical knowledge that would have been required. This all points out the importance of things celestial to Shakespeare and his fellow players, as well as signaling the imaginative power of heavenly objects among their audiences.

Shakespeare was amazingly sensitive to the fabric of his times, and wove that fabric throughout his works. The calendar was an intrinsic part of that fabric, and with its related issues of astronomy, astrology, Catholicism, and politics, it stood out as a central issue of the day. Given all that, it seems pretty apparent that Will had the sources, knowledge, understanding, and inclination to use it as an ongoing subject and structure in *Hamlet* and in the rest of his works.

Yond Same Star That's Westward from the Pole

At the risk of dancing on pinheads, I'd like to take a closer look at an item in Chapter One that some readers may agree bears further discussion: Steve Sohmer's identification of Bernardo's star as Deneb. While his discussion of Deneb and the Northern Cross is quite persuasive, other possibilities have been raised in the past, and are summarized in a 1998 *Sky and Telescope* article entitled "The Stars of Hamlet." The authors, Olson, Olson, and Doescher (who I'll refer to as "the Olsons") rule out several possibilities that have been raised in the past, including Deneb, on the grounds that those stars are not "westward of the pole" at one AM in early November. (They agree with Sohmer, and me, in placing the opening scenes around that time.)

The Olsons state that Cassiopeia is in the right position relative to Polaris—"with nearly the same altitude...on the 'west' side (or 'to the left') of the pole"—at one AM during that time of year. But since Cassiopeia contains no bright stars, they suggest that Bernardo's star is the supernova that appeared in Cassiopeia in early November of 1572, which was commented upon by both Tycho Brahe on November 11 and later by Thomas Digges. Given the relationship between *Hamlet,* Brahe, and Digges that the Olsons and Usher argue for so persuasively (see Appendix D), it's not a bad surmise. (Usher's subsequent suggestion that the action of *Hamlet* runs from 1572 to 1576 is unsupportable; as demonstrated in Chapter Two, the action encompasses only four months.)

Before accepting the Olsons' identification of the star, though, I'd like to return to the method they used to rule out Deneb and other stars. Their primary reason for dismissing them is that they were not directly westward of the pole at the right time. Let's get Bernardo's full statement in front of us for review. 1.1.35

> Last night of all,
> When yond same star that's westward from the pole
> Had made his course t' illumine that part of heaven
> Where now it burns, Marcellus and myself,
> The bell then beating one—
>   *Enter Ghost*

Next, let's take a moment to analyze the key items that give clues as to which star Bernardo might be pointing out (if any). There are three key questions:

- On what date is Bernardo speaking?
- What time is it?
- What does "westward from the pole" mean?

The evidence for early November is cited by both Sohmer and the Olsons: it's "bitter cold," it's before or after Advent, and two months prior, Old Hamlet was napping in his garden. So late October or early November seems likely. Sohmer asserts the morning of November 2, All Soul's Day. The Olsons opt for November 11th, the date that Brahe first saw the supernova.

As to the time, there's some ambiguity in the text. The time sequence in both rampart scenes is accelerated, going from around midnight to dawn in the course of the scenes. This is especially true in the first. At line seven it's just after midnight ("'Tis now strook twelf" 1.1.7). When Bernardo points out the star thirty-one lines later it is (perhaps) one o'clock. And only a hundred lines after that, the cock crows the dawn. So much for unity of time. The elastic nature of time in the scene is emphasized later, when Horatio and the guards report to Hamlet: 1.2.236

Hamlet: Stay'd it long?

Horatio: While one with moderate haste might tell a hundreth.

Marcellus and Bernardo: Longer, longer.

Horatio: Not when I saw't.

(I am at a loss as to the purpose of this odd little contretemps—aside from emphasizing the subjective nature of time—and would welcome suggestions.) My best guess is that when Bernardo points out the star, it is just after midnight; it was on the *previous* night that the ghost appeared when the bell was beating one. (The ghost arrives before midnight on his fourth visit, as explained in Chapter Two; he seems to be impatient, arriving earlier each night.) The ghost appears on the heels of Bernardo's line, then disappears, and then Marcellus tells us "Thus twice before, and jump at this dead hour/...hath he gone by our watch." 1.1.65 This suggests that it's exactly the same time as the previous night—one o'clock.

So there's contradiction in the text, revolving around how quickly time is passing in the scene. But we can say that the star reference happens between midnight and one.

Now as to the meaning of "westward from the pole." First, Bernardo is not so absolute a knave as the gravedigger; his "that part of heaven" seems to add quite a bit of leeway as to the star's exact position. My take is that the star is generally westward of the pole, and that it's generally in the same part of the sky as it was the previous night.

But what does "westward" mean? The Olsons suggest that it means "to the left" of Polaris, at the same altitude above the horizon. But it could also mean "on the line from Polaris to the western horizon," which would put the star at a lower altitude, to the left of but "below" Polaris. (I reviewed usages of "pole" by Shakespeare and his contemporaries, and it seems clear that Bernardo's reference *is* to Polaris, not to the northern horizon.)

At this point we should take a look at the night sky at the time in question, as the Olsons don't provide a diagram, and the illustration accompanying Sohmer's article is somewhat difficult to interpret for non-astronomers.

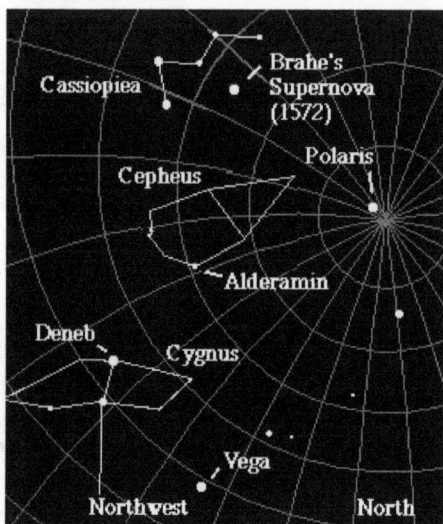

The northwestern sky from London at one minute past midnight on November 2, 1601. (The view from Denmark is almost identical.) The horizon is at the bottom. At one AM the constellations will have rotated downward, counterclockwise, by fifteen degrees. For simplicity, this chart shows only those stars of magnitude 3 or less. (Lower magnitude numbers are brighter. Vega is the brightest on this chart, with magnitude 0.)

As you learned in grade school, of course, the image above is a section of an empty grapefruit half, smashed onto the page using a projection method first developed in Shakespeare's time. That makes it hard to visualize what the sky actually looked like. So try the following exercise.

1. Pretend it's just after midnight on the morning on November 2, 1601. You're standing on the ramparts of Elsinore, looking north. The full moon is behind you, about 60 degrees above the horizon. Directly in front of you is Polaris, the north star, 53 degrees above the horizon. (The horizon is at 0 degrees; 90 degrees is straight up.)

2. Hold both arms straight out in front of you, pointing up at Polaris.

3. Leaving your right hand stationary, move your left arm across to the left, keeping it at the same height, until it's pointing northwest.

4. Drop your left arm so it's aiming 26 degrees above the horizon. You're pointing at Deneb.

5. Raise your left hand to 65 degrees above the horizon and to the right a skootch. You're pointing at the center of Cassiopeia.

6. Between these two, at about 49 degrees, you're pointing at the center of the constellation Cepheus (about which more anon).

Deneb, being so low in the sky, is a bit hard to describe as "to the left" of Polaris. But it is in a direct line from Polaris to the western horizon, which I think Bernardo would credit when he says "westward from the pole." Cassiopeia really seems above and to the left. I would subscribe to it in a pinch.

The only star I can see above magnitude 3 that's pretty much "to the left" of Polaris is Alderamin. It's only magnitude 2.4, which makes it questionable to think Bernardo would pick it out, but that's a pretty empty part of the sky, so it does stand out some. It's the brightest star in the constellation Cepheus—"the king" and head of the royal family that includes Cassiopeia and Andromeda. Cepheus is spoken of as having Polaris as his footstool. And Bernardo's reference to "*his* course" makes Cepheus somewhat more likely than Cassiopeia (though "his" and "its" were used somewhat interchangeably by Elizabethans).

Cepheus Rising

In fact, though, Cepheus didn't seem much of a prospect until I came across the following discussion of Cepheus rising in Marcus Manilius' *Astronomicon*, a first-century Roman astronomical and astrological discourse that was rediscovered during the renaissance. I've added paragraph breaks for easier reading; the original Latin is in verse. (G. P. Goold translation, lines 449–485. I've posted a 1675 verse translation and the original Latin at princehamlet.com.)

But Cepheus, rising beside the dripping Waterman [Aquarius], will not engender dispositions inclined to sport. He fashions faces marked by a stern demeanour, and moulds a countenance whereon is depicted gravity of mind. Such men will live on worry and will

incessantly recall the traditions of a bygone age and commend old
Cato's maxims.

Cepheus will also create a man to bring up boys of tender age:
he will lord it over his lord by virtue of the law which governs a
minor and, bemused by this semblance of power, will mistake for
reality the role of arrogant guardian or stern uncle which he plays.

Offspring of Cepheus will also furnish words for the buskin of
tragedy, [Goold's note: On the Farnese globe Cepheus is depicted
in the garb of a tragic actor. My note: This depiction was mimicked
on globes extant in Elizabethan England.] whose pen, if only on
paper, is drenched in blood; and the paper no less [Goold: Than
the audience at a performance] will revel in the spectacle of crime
and catastrophe in human affairs.

They will delight to tell of scarce one burial accorded three:
the father belching forth the flesh of his sons, the sun fled in hor
ror, and the darkness of a cloudless day; they will delight to narrate
the Theban war between a mother's issue, and one who was both
father and brother to his children; the story of Medea's sons, her
brother and her father, the gift which was first robe and then con-
suming flame, the escape by air, and youth reborn from fire. A
thousand other scenes from the past will they include in their
plays; perhaps Cepheus himself will also be brought upon the
stage.

If anyone is born with the urge to write in lighter vein, he will
compose for presentation at the merry games scenes of comedy
about the loves of headstrong youths and abducted maidens,
hoodwinked old men, and slaves of infinite resource. In such plays
Menander made his own day live for all generations: a man whose
eloquence surpassed that of his native Atherns (and that when its
language attained its richest bloom), he held up a mirror to life and
enshrined the image in his works.

Should his powers not rise to such masterpieces, the child of
Cepheus will yet be fitted to perform those of others: he will interpret the poet's words, now by his voice, now by silent gesture and
expression, and the lines he declaims he will make his own. On the
stage he will take the part of Romans or the mighty heroes of myth;
he will assume every role himself, one after another, and in his sin-

gle person represent a crowd; he will draw over his limbs the aspect
of fortune's every vicissitude and his gestures will match the songs
of the chorus; he will convince you that you see Troy's actual fall
and Priam expiring before your very eyes.

Oddly enough, the first passage rings strongly of Claudius. (Cepheus is
"the king," after all.) But the remainder reads more like a description of
Shakespeare. I'll just note two of these correlations.

- "held up a mirror up to life," and its similarity to Hamlet's words when
advising the First Player.

    "...with this special observance, that you o'erstep not the modesty
    of nature: for any thing so o'erdone is from the purpose of playing,
    whose end, both at the first and now, was and is, to hold as 'twere
    the mirror up to nature: to show virtue her feature, scorn her own
    image, and the very age and body of the time his form and pres-
    sure." 3.2.18

- "he will convince you that you see Troy's actual fall and Priam expiring
before your very eyes" cannot but make a Hamlet reader think of the
Hecuba speech 2.2.450, which describes exactly that.

It's clear that Goold, the translator, knew his Shakespeare, and may well
have found there his "mirror" there. But the remainder, so obviously reminiscent of Shakespeare regardless of language, could have influenced *Hamlet*'s author.

Did Shakespeare know *Astronomicon*? Given the breadth and selection of
material we know he did read, it seems more than just likely. Latin editions
were published in 1579, 1590, and 1600, edited and annotated by a French
philologist and historian—later a professor at Leyden in the low countries—
named Joseph Justus Scaliger (1540-1609). Scaliger was one of the best-
known scholars of the day, with many references to him—and many more to
his father's *Poetics*—in the late sixteenth century. Sidney refers extensively to
both Scaligers in the *Defense of Poesie* (written ca. 1579, published 1595).
Ben Jonson even has a character joking about him in his *Every Man Out of
His Humour*, which Shakespeare's company performed in a revised form
containing the following passage, in 1600. Clove, aping scholarly discourse,

says, "Aristotle in his daemonologia approves Scaliger for the best navigator in his time, and in his hypercritics he reports him to be Heautontimorumenos!" (He then spouts a bunch of faux astronomy-speak, aimed, obviously, not at the pit but at the savants in the galleries.)

And Scaliger was right in the thick of the whole astronomy/calendar business of the day, including correspondence with Henry Savile, one of the calendar consultants to Elizabeth and Burghley discussed in Appendix D. In addition to *Astronomicon*, Scaliger's 1583 *Study on the Improvement of Time* reviewed the calendar methods of the past, and invented the system of "Julian days" that's still used today as the astronomical standard (the system—distinct from the Julian calendar—is actually named after his father, Julius Caesar Scaliger). And the younger Scaliger's 1609 *The Thesaurus of Time, Including the Chronicle of Eusebius Pamphilus* set forth a chronological method that formed the foundation for modern study of ancient history. It's an interesting connection, given the chronological and astronomical fixation in *Hamlet*.

But to return to the matter: If you combine the location of Cepheus at the time in question, Bernardo's reference to "his course," the connections between *Hamlet,* Shakespeare, and the Cepheus material in Manilius/Scaliger's *Astronomicon,* and the likelihood that Shakespeare had seen this material, then Cepheus with its brightest star, Alderamin, starts to look like a pretty attractive candidate for Bernardo to be referring to.

One final item before leaving this topic: In researching it I had the opportunity to examine the large collection of celestial globes at the Greenwich Maritime Museum—including one that was on display at the time, on loan from the Middle Temple (with its manifold connections to Shakespeare, nicely explicated in Anthony Alridge's *Shakespeare and the Prince of Love: The Feast of Misrule in the Middle Temple*). On that globe, Alderamin is rubbed off—apparently by being touched many times by many fingers. There is no such marring anywhere else on the globe, which is in excellent condition. I have no explanation for this, only curiosity.

It's certainly possible, of course, that Bernardo's star is just a poetic construct, with no actual counterpart in the celestial sphere. Sometimes a star is just a star. But given the many astronomical connections in *Hamlet* and the importance of astrology in Elizabethan England (detailed in Appendix D), an allusion to either Deneb in Cygnus/Northern Cross or Alderamin in Cepheus is a likely conjecture.

The Drowning of Katherine Hamlett

In Chapter Two I briefly discussed Katherine Hamlett, who drowned in the Avon near Stratford on December 17, 1579 (when Shakespeare was 15), and the relationship between her final burial date and my proposed chronology for *Hamlet*. I also alluded to the similarities between Katherine's case and Ophelia's, which similarities have been noted by various authors and editors. In this appendix I'd like to explore those connections in more detail (because it's fascinating and sometimes funny stuff), and in the process, I hope, provide more support for my suggested burial date of February 14.

The key connection is the discussion of voluntary suicide versus accidental death, and whether the deceased can receive a full Christian burial. In his 1885 *Ecclesiastical Law in Hamlet: The Burial of Ophelia*, R. A. Guernsey gives a very complete explanation of burial rites for suicides as prescribed in the Elizabethan church, their relation to secular law, and their manifestation in the graveyard scene. He says, in fact, that "in Hamlet can be found allusions and statements showing the most thorough and complete knowledge of the canon and statute law of England, relating to the burial of suicides, that has ever been written." Better than Blackstone, better than Coke. High praise, that, for a noverint scrivener.

Guernsey explains that a coroner's inquest into a possible suicide (a secular affair) held sway over ecclesiastical authorities; it determined whether the deceased could receive Christian burial. If the finding was voluntary suicide, "the body was denied the church rites of burial and was buried by the coroner according to the local custom of the parish." One custom was burial at a crossroads, outside the hallowed ground of the churchyard, where passersby were encouraged to throw stones at the gravesite (this drawing on fairly barbaric customs of the Teutons for execution of criminals at crossroads). "But that great command o'ersways the order...Shards, flints, and pebbles should be thrown on her." 5.1.231

If the coroner's inquest determined that the suicide was a result of insanity, the coroner released the body to the parish priest; the body might be buried within the churchyard, with the place to be selected by the priest. Many churches had areas on the extreme north verge of the graveyard, where were buried "suicides, still-born infants, and excommunicated persons." Some of these graves do not run east-west (in line with the church, and in line with accepted practices for Christian burial). This is what the gravediggers are saying when they talk about making Ophelia's grave "straight" in their opening lines: 5.1.1

> 1. Clo. Is she to be buried in Christian burial when she willfully seeks her own salvation?
>
> 2. Clo. I tell thee she is, therefore make her grave straight. The crowner hath sate on her, and finds it Christian burial.

If the coroner's inquest returned a verdict of accident rather than suicide (intentional or insane), the parish priest—however churlish—was required to accede to those conclusions and provide Christian burial. As we'll see in a moment, though, the priest had some discretion even then.

To Act, To Do, To Perform

Guernsey didn't know about Kate Hamlett, but he discusses the case of Sir James Hales, who in Mary's reign committed suicide by throwing himself into a stream. The ensuing court case was reported in the lawyer Edmund

Plowden's *Reports*, of which four editions were published in London between 1571 and 1599. The languge of the court case is amusing both in its
legal quiddities and in its remarkable similarities to the clown's shredding of
legal language.

A certain Sergeant Walsh, arguing that Hales did not complete the suicide
during his lifetime, asserted that suicide consists of three parts:

> 1. The imagination, which is a reflection or meditation of the mind
> whether or not it is convenient to destroy himself....
>
> 2. The resolution, which is a determination of the mind to destroy
> himself...
>
> 3. The perfection, which is the execution of what the mind has re-
> solved to do.

The gravedigger, legal scholar that he is, echoes this: "if I drown myself
wittingly, it argues an act, and an act hath three branches—it is, to act, to do,
to perform; argal, she drown'd herself wittingly." Continuing his cogent
analysis, he says:

> 1. Clo. Here lies the water; good. Here stands the man; good. If the
> man go to this water and drown himself, it is, will he, nill he, he
> goes, mark you that. But if the water come to him and drown him,
> he drowns not himself; argal, he that is not guilty of his own death
> shortens not his own life.
>
> 2. Clo. But is this law?
>
> 1. Clo. Ay, mary, is't—crowner's quest law.

This is an amusing though not exact parody, actually going one better
than Judge Brown's stirring conclusion in the Hales case:

> Sir James Hales was dead, and how came he to his death? It may be
> answered by drowning—and who drowned him? Sir James
> Hales—and when did he drown him? In his life time. So that Sir
> James Hales being alive caused Sir James Hales to die! And the act

of the living man was the death of the dead man. And then for this offence it is reasonable to punish the living man who commited the offence, and not the dead man. But how can he be said to be punished alive when the punishment comes after his death?

Chief Justice Dyer added:

> All the Justices agreed that the foreiture of the goods and chattels real and personal of Sir James Hales shall have relation to the act done in his life-time, which was the cause of his death, viz: the throwing himself into the water.

Maimed Rites

The rites to be performed at a Christian burial are yet another issue. The essential ritual was laid out clearly in the 1559 *Book of Common Prayer,* but Guernsey explains that these are only the minimum rites. Different parishes might have different customs, some drawing on the old Catholic rituals. This is what Hamlet comments upon and Laertes objects to: 5.1.218

> Hamlet: The Queen, the courtiers. Who is this they follow?
> And with such maimed rites? This doth betoken
> The corse they follow did with desp'rate hand
> Foredo it own life. 'Twas of some estate.
> Couch we a while and mark.
>
> Laertes: What ceremony else?
>
> Hamlet: That is Laertes, a very noble youth. Mark.
>
> Laertes: What ceremony else?
>
> Doctor. Her obsequies have been as far enlarg'd
> As we have warranty. Her death was doubtful,
> And but that great command o'ersways the order,
> She should in ground unsanctified been lodg'd
> Till the last trumpet; for charitable prayers,
> Shards, flints, and pebbles should be thrown on her.

Yet here she is allow'd her vergin crants,
Her maiden strewments, and the bringing home
Of bell and burial.

Laertes: Must there no more be done?

Doctor: No more be done:
We should profane the service of the dead
To sing a requiem and such rest to her
As to peace-parted souls.

Laertes: Lay her i' th' earth,
And from her fair and unpolluted flesh
May violets spring! I tell thee, churlish priest,
A minist'ring angel shall my sister be
When thou liest howling.

The coroner's inquest has brought in a judgment of accidental death, so Ophelia is to be buried in hallowed ground, with "straight" grave, and she's to be strewed with flowers rather than rained with rocks. But the priest believes the death "doubtful"—that the finding is the result of "great command" which "o'ersways the order." (Coroners were in service to the crown, as emphasized by the clown's pronunciation: "crowner.") The priest only performs the minimum ritual—no requiem sung—and that grudgingly.

A Dead Woman in Tiddington

Having received this instruction in canon and statute law from Shakespeare, the gravedigger, and Dr. Guernsey, you have to ask (or I do, in any case) how it all relates to the drowning of Katherine Hamlett, spinster. Here's the full report of the coroner's inquest into Katherine's death, as translated from the Latin by Edgar Fripp in *Minutes and Accounts of the Corporation of Stratford-Upon-Avon* (1926):

Warwick.
Inquisition indented taken at Tiddington in the County aforesaid on the eleventh day of February in the twenty-second year of the reign of our Lady Elizabeth, by the grace of God Queen of Eng-

land, France and Ireland, defender of the Faith &c. before Henry
Rogers, a coroner of the said lady of the Queen in the County
aforesaid, on a view of the body of Katherine Hamlett, late of Tiddington aforesaid in the County aforesaid, spinster, found there
dead and drowned, on the oath of John Pearse, thomas Townsend,
Giles Walker, Edmund Baker, Thomas Baker, Richard Godwine,
William Fawkener, John Lord, Thomas Givves, thomas Hickes,
Thomas Warde, Robert Simcocks and Robert Griffine : Who say
on their oath that the aforesaid Katherin Hamlett, on the seventeenth day of December in the twenty-second year of the reign of
the aforesaid lady the Queen, going with a certain vessel, in English
a Pail, to draw water at the river called Avon in Tiddington afore
said, it so happened that the aforesaid Katherine, standing on the
bank of the same river, suddenly and by accident slipped and fell
into the river aforesaid, and there, in the water of the same river on
the said seventeenth day of December in the year aforesaid at Tiddington aforesaid in the County aforesaid by accident was
drowned, and not otherwise nor in other fashion came by her
death. In testimony whereof both the coroner aforesaid and the
jury aforesaid have set their seal to this inquisition indented on the
day, in the year, and in the place abovesaid.

    By accident.

Unfortunately we don't know any more than this. There's no record of
Kate's burial, because the key page from the Alveston parish register (Tiddington is included in that parish)—covering February 15, 1579 to April 14
1582—was torn out at some time prior to 1930, when Fripp reported it
missing. We can draw several conclusions from the report, though, and from
the standard practices of coroner's inquests.

First, Kate's body was "on a view" at the inquest. This was standard
wording and practice (true *habeus corpus*), not releasing the body to the
relatives or the parish priest until the inquest was complete. Almost identical
wording was used, for instance (choosing a famous example), at the inquest
into Christopher Marlowe's death on the day after his stabbing, in 1593.

But in Kate's case, *eight weeks* had passed since her death. Either she was
buried then exhumed, or her body was held somewhere and somehow.

The other key item from the inquest is its unequivocal finding "By accident." This, and the inquest itself, make clear that there was some question as to her death, a question sufficient to hold up her burial for eight weeks. Perhaps the question arose from Alveston's churlish priest, and the family objected, requesting an inquest so they could give Kate proper burial. In any case, the body would have been released on the day of the inquest, Thursday, February 11, or perhaps the day after. Given how long it had been since her death, there would not have been great hurry to get her in the ground. After their long wait, it would have been natural for the family to have waited until the following Sunday February 14, Shrove Sunday, to bury Kate with full rites and rituals.

Whatever the exact series of events, the drowning, inquest, and long-delayed burial would have excited no little comment and discussion among the townsfolk, and Shakespeare would have been hard-pressed not to hear of it. There were only about 1,500 souls in Stratford at the time. Henry Rogers the coroner was the town clerk. And only a dozen years past, Will's father John had been bailiff of Stratford, the town's highest office. I can't share Fripp's impetuous notion that "Shakespeare was probably in Roger's office when....the inquest was held," but it seems almost certain that 15-year-old Will knew the case, if not the affected party.

About the Author

Steve Roth took his BA in Literature, Theory and Criticism from Western Washington University, and received his MA from New York University under the Oscar Dystel Fellowship, endowed by Bantam Books. He's written, edited, and/or produced dozens of books, and has been a writer and editor for several magazines, including *Publishers Weekly, Personal Publishing, Macworld,* and *Small Press.* He's been involved with various publishing startups, and in 1991 he co-founded Thunder Lizard Productions, where he spent nine years as president and CEO. He lives in Seattle with his two daughters. His Shakespeare scholarship includes papers presented at a variety of international conferences, and articles in *Early Modern Literary Studies, Notes & Queries,* and *Ben Jonson Journal,* all available at princehamlet.com.

9780970470218